Orange Juice and Oil

Memoirs of a Baby Boomer

Peter Morley

Perfect ublishers Ltd

REVISED EDITION

ISBN: 978-1-905399-72-7

Paperback

Cover Design by Duncan Bamford
http://www.insightillustration.co.uk

Edited by Jan Andersen
http://www.creativecopywriter.org

PERFECT PUBLISHERS LTD
23 Maitland Avenue
Cambridge
CB4 1TA
England
http://www.perfectpublishers.co.uk

Dedication

This book is dedicated to my parents, Molly and George Morley, and all the decent, reliable people in the world who have worked to build the society we now enjoy. It is written for my children and grandchildren to help them understand and cherish what they have inherited.

Acknowledgements

I wrote this book because I wanted to record my experiences, and the thoughts and ideas they inspired, for my grandchildren so they might know something of their grandfather and of an age not so long ago but rather different from theirs.

The book has been worth writing just for the experience of working with some caring, passionate people, and I need to thank them for their parts in it. I did not expect to write a publishable book until Terrie Rintoul found a little talent for writing somewhere in me. I am grateful that she ignored my entreaties to be honest and, instead, encouraged me. The team at Perfect Publishers have deserved their name and I have appreciated their professionalism and enthusiasm. My wife, Rosie, and my children, in whom I am blessed, need to be acknowledged for their patient proofreading and helpful comments, as do friends Rog and Maz Williams who helped me over some of the frailties of my memory, and Jenny Mugridge who kindly provided comments on the manuscript.

I have led a charmed life thanks to Rosie who has ignored my faults and made me a king. When was an undeserving fellow ever made to feel more able? Also, I have been improved by a number of worthwhile people, including teachers at my country schools, who gave me a sufficient base to build on; I was inspired, at formative moments, to be as good an engineer as I could possibly be by knowledgeable and generous individuals who crossed my path; and it has been my good fortune to have worked for some effective bosses in Britain and America, who were flexible enough to accept me and offer opportunities I could grasp.

Above all, my thanks go to the brilliant and committed people I have had the privilege to lead. My greatest success was learning that a manager's job is to gather good people together, create an environment in which they can be successful and let them do the rest.

Disclaimer

All personal events described within this book are true, or as true as the veracity of the author's memory allows. However, some names have been changed or omitted and, generally, the names of work colleagues mentioned in this book have been changed in order to protect identities.

Revised Edition

Even a lifetime later some memories can be sensitive. The revised edition makes some changes in respect of this.

Author Biography

Peter Morley is a Chartered Engineer, family man and rower. Orange Juice and Cod Liver Oil is his first book, written a year after retiring from 45 years of working in engineering and thinking about the social order. He was born in 1946, in the coldest winter on record, and grew up in a post-war Britain of bomb craters, ration books and National Health orange juice and cod liver oil.

An 11+ failure, educated at small country schools and in a 5-year apprenticeship, he eventually obtained an engineering degree as a part-time student and went on to work as design engineer, project manager and group manager of a world class team, designing and building process plants for the production of hydrogen and other industrial gases.

As a young man he found his soul mate, they married and together brought up four children who have so far given them seven grandchildren.

Contents

Preface

It's a Beautiful World

They sat in a grassy clearing not far from the river, enjoying the sun's warmth and absorbing its energy. The clean, musky smell of the browning grasses and bracken added comfort to their contentment. They had no need of conversation in that moment and the riparian sounds at that wood's edge drifted into their senses: the ripple of water accelerating across the rocky cataract, insects lazily about the late flowers and the light breeze just disturbing the stiffening leaves of the trees around them. These great trees that seemed not to have changed in all the summers they had been together; perhaps not in all the summers they had known.

Life felt good at this time of year with such a variety of berries, fruit and nuts, just there for the taking, and dry wood so easy to gather for the fire now that the days were shortening; although all their senses and everything they knew told them they were just temporary visitors to this reliable, constant world.

They were happy; grateful just to have a part, for longer than that of the brimstone butterfly skipping toward the scent of the honeysuckle, but shorter than that of the mighty oak that guarded the valley. It all seemed to be there for their use and their pleasure. It might be interesting to understand why it was this way, but it didn't really matter.

Reluctant to break the silence, to encroach on the bucolic idyll, but needing to air what was bothering him, he pushed aside the hair from her neck with his nose and said softly, "Evie," and again, with a timid kiss, "Evie, I've been thinking about what you said – about settling down. I love you dearly; you have given me four sons and I think the world of you, but I think there's a lot to be said for hunter gathering.

"I know people are saying we could have more corn by planting the seed and they think those flightless birds seem friendly enough to be persuaded to lay their eggs in a box for us to use – if we fed them. But it would be a lot of work to clear the ground and I know whose job *that* would be.

"Look at it this way; we are healthy, thanks to the seasonal variation that gives us a balanced diet. If we move to staples such as that starchy corn stuff, for example, we will not be getting *all* the vitamins we need. I think it's safer to stick to a natural diet.

"And look what happened – what they say happened – when people in the three rivers area stopped moving for two summers. They got sick and some died. As soon as they got back on the move they were fine. And we're fine. Yes, I know Eric and Paul got eaten by bears, but the other two children are tall and healthy. On balance it's better to lose a few to wild animals than risk unbalancing the lifestyle we have.

"And if we settle down we'll get specialisation and you know what that means: some people will tell us they add more value by making trading tokens, or something, and give themselves extra rations.

"And people will have time to talk; youngsters will learn from the elders, get educated and then start thinking. I don't think... I don't think that would be healthy.

"I've heard that, quite a few summers ago, some people thought they needed a Special Being, something bigger than themselves, something to look up to, to set down some rules. And you know what happened; they got specialists - Special Being specialists - who just sat around thinking and making wise sayings while others brought them food. Wise sayings that weren't so wise when people actually understood what they were talking about.

"It's not the Special Being that bothers me; life can be a bit daunting sometimes and it would be good to have someone to talk things over with. It's the middlemen; they're bound to arrange things for their own advantage.

"Then we'll think we need leaders and we'll have to decide who. There'll be favouritism and people will do things just to get a better cave or more land. And when they die, their sons will expect to keep the land, even if *they* haven't worked for it.

"The hand axe is a great innovation but I don't think we should push it. It's dangerous to interfere with nature.

"We don't own anything, haven't got rights; just responsibilities and things work well. You have to prove yourself every day and that's the way it should be. You're only as good as your last success."

"And when was your last success? You're supposed to be a hunter." Evie thought she had heard enough.

"I do, ok. I hunt and you gather; it's a good life."

"Yes, but you never catch anything."

"I caught a salmon last year when the river was low. You enjoyed that; would have been better if you hadn't overcooked it, granted."

"I don't get much practice. If you caught them more often I could develop some recipes, add a few herbs and berries. I'd like time to be creative at the fire. And you know why the river was low; my mother says there's another ice age coming. We had better prepare; settling down would enable us to store food and we could build our own cave with a proper fireplace and she could live with us. She's finding it harder to keep up these days, when we are on the move."

"That's another good reason. And, if the bears eat her, there may be a chance they would leave the boys alone; long enough for them to grow up. Nature might seem hard sometimes, but it knows what it's doing."

"You'll never amount to anything – just hunting – and not usually catching anything. *And* you never lift a finger around the cave."

"I've got my art."

"A few ochre scratchings on the cave wall where no one can see them isn't art and, anyway, mammoths don't do *that*."

"But Evie, now we're all equal and free and we don't owe anything and our children won't inherit any debt. I think we should leave it, at least for a few more summers."

"I'm not going to leave it there, Ad. I'm not lying with you again until it's in a permanent bed. You've had a good run but I'm putting my foot down."

"You're so unreasonable sometimes. I suppose…"

"Oh, cum on Ad, have an apple: it'll be fine…"

This is one idea of how the present phase of our evolution, the social phase, may have begun. We have made progress in social evolution and, although there have been many mistakes, we seem to be advancing towards a society in which, increasingly, there is respect and opportunity for more people. We are learning how to use democracy and, cautiously, how to let go of the elitism and privilege that gave dynamism to the industrial age.

Throughout my life, between surviving, learning, providing, competing and loving, I have sought to interpret the available data in order to discover who I am and why I am here. I think this is normal in our species, gifted with intelligence and driven by curiosity.

Just an Ordinary Family

What follows is the story of just one family among the millions of ordinary, but remarkable, human families. Human families carry in their genes and inherited ideas all the pain and joy, failure and triumph, fear and hope experienced throughout their history. I am the product of one family and their history; my parts are distilled from the genes of my parents, flavoured by the experiences of my own life and matured in the times through which I have lived. The only way for me to understand who I am is to understand where I have come from. The legacies I offer my children depend on this history and on the influences I expose them to – or protect them from.

The Oxford dictionary defines history as a chronological record of important or public events, but the history that helps each of us to understand who we are and where we have come from is in the experiences of our people, with the emotions that sustained them and forged their characters.

This is the story of my family through its last few generations and is similar to that of countless others. Some families will be linked directly to dramatic public events or famous people, but while such things may add colour, they probably do not increase the character or value of one individual over another. We all belong to a very special species living on a remarkable planet in an exciting time. What we choose to do with our inheritance is down to each of us and understanding our own story could be an important part in the choosing.

We learn, especially from our parents and those with whom we spend our time, absorbing knowledge, ideas and feelings. Much of this is positive, especially if we are lucky enough to live in an enlightened and supportive community.

Even in good circumstances, however, we probably absorb some unhealthy ideas. In some cases whole communities carry reactionary feelings and prejudices that colour objectivity.

It is possibly due to an aspect of our evolution forged in our Darwinian survival-of-the-fittest tribal past that we favour our own people's views and oppose those of others. Although this may have once contributed to a successful survival strategy, it can make us resistant and blinkered to the ideas of others with different histories. If civilisation is to lift itself to a higher plane, we will need to look for the good in everyone and the weaknesses in ourselves while understanding and managing our differences.

The history of our society throughout its industrial period is a history of innovation, freedom to be enterprising, establishment of privilege, corruption, exploitation, struggle for emancipation and social adjustment; all this occurring in cycles, partially repeating earlier situations, but gradually advancing to a fairer, more prosperous and fulfilling world available to more people. We are making progress.

In Britain we are all fortunate to live in the place that has been centre of the advancement of civilisation over the last millennium and, whilst a privileged minority have achieved social positions that have enabled them to influence and exploit the rest of the population, we have all ultimately benefitted from the advancements in industry, commerce, knowledge and education.

So far, so good.

Chapter 1

The End

On an August morning in 2009, it came to an end. It just stopped; ceased to be. That life, powered by its indomitable spirit had gone, had its day; passed on.

Life carries the spirit, yet it is the spirit that powers the life. Actually, this life had carried two spirits for its last thirty two and a half years: those of my mother and my father. My mother, Molly Morley, had carried my father's memory so faithfully that his spirit had seemed to live on in her – with hers. And those two spirits were a force to be reckoned with. Either, on its own, had seemed to be robust, but the combination was truly wonderful. Such was the thing that was made and grew when those two lives came together, each having sustained itself through adversity, disappointment and injustice.

When they came together there was more than empathy, understanding and respect; there was an affinity and mutual need that grew into a great and indivisible love. It welded the two spirits into one and would see them rise from the ashes of war and unpromising beginnings to become a family with moral strength and the determination that would drive them through life, accepting every opportunity, no matter how small and repelling every challenge, no matter how great. And there were challenges.

He was big, strong and courageous, yet weakened by the war, a broken marriage and strained family relationships. Guided - perhaps bullied even - and challenged by a father himself damaged physically and mentally by his own war and turned on by a sister whom he had loved, but who had lost her way through too much beauty, too much success and too many rich husbands.

His show business marriage had failed when his first wife ran off with another to Canada, leaving him with a young son.

My Mother was small and vulnerable and, with a hard childhood not long behind her, she felt she needed to escape from a home with few comforts. She was ready to take the chance of marrying a man with whom there could be the hope of a better life.

Chapter 2

Country Ways and Troubled Times

My mother was from a farming family on her father's side that had been in the New Forest for at least three generations before her. Mum loved the Forest in a way that was more than just a regard for its scenery. To hear her talk, she was part of it and when she was away it seemed to draw her back. In later life, even on a visit to me in the next county, her demeanour would change and she would relax when we crossed the first cattle grid on the return journey.

Mum's father was not attentive to his family. His father had died when he was 14, just when the guidance of a father would have been important, his teenage years had been spent under the cloud of the Great War, in which his older brother served, and he had received an inheritance rather easily. Perhaps these were not the best conditions for him to learn about responsibility.

His father, my great-grandfather had 11 children, only 5 of whom survived infancy, with his first wife. In 1896, the year after she died, he married his young housekeeper and they went on to have 13 children in their marriage, 10 of whom survived.

My great-grandfather made his living from the land and the forest. He may have thought he had Commoners' rights to graze his animals, but records show him frequently in court for having cattle loose, also for poaching, although he became a bailiff in later life (a poacher turned gamekeeper).

He was a resourceful man and had enough flair and drive to progress. Official records show that he accumulated a substantial amount of property. Today, it may seem surprising that he managed this without being able to sign his name. The legal documents I have seen show his mark, witnessed by a solicitor.

He provided casual employment for local people on his property and, to speed the movement of produce from his land to market, built two roads. These are in use today as part of the New Forest road network.

He seems to have been something of an opportunist. From family folklore, he had accumulated at least some of his wealth from the practice of lending money to local people in distress in return for the deeds of their property, such that it fell into his ownership on their deaths. This may sound like a form of usury, but is not very different from that practised by some of our most "respectable" financial institutions today.

It is said that he sent his children to church regularly and made efforts to set his family in a positive direction.

My great-grandfather did not practise the old money principle of primogeniture and, in his will, distributed his land among his children. He provided contiguous smallholdings for the boys, except the youngest who had been born after his death, in the hope that they would farm the land cooperatively. They did not; their holdings were not viable on their own and my grandfather did not manage to keep his property.

The proceeds of the sale of the two other estates owned by my great-grandfather were left to his daughters and his wife.

Mum's mother came from a village in Kerry. She had moved to Cork City to work as a domestic servant for a bank manager where she met my grandfather who was serving in the British army. I think she came from ordinary Irish country family with a fairly typical history. Her sisters had emigrated to Boston, Massachusetts and a brother had gone to live in New Zealand. This was during the Irish War of Independence, euphemistically referred to as "The Troubles".

After the First World War the reform movement in Ireland, which had previously been progressed mainly by political means, was marginalised by the anarchy of terrorism. Those who were able to, left the country. Most migrated to Britain in this period, which seems to confirm that the Irish are not inherently anti-British. These were decent people looking for a life away from conflict and they reluctantly abandoned their country when they saw it destroyed by bitterness and corruption. Left behind were the thugs who now led the agenda; the clerics who had their own motives and those unable to escape.

Irish history is hard to understand perhaps because it is usually told by those closest and with the strongest emotional connection to it. For those further away it has many intertwined threads that are difficult to untangle and to try to do so risks opening the wounds, never completely healed, which were inflicted by the violence.

Our social evolution has been interrupted by many conflicts in which the dark side of our nature is exposed and enables us to destroy one another. Although we will continue to disgrace ourselves by allowing such mistakes, our adaptability enables us to learn a little each time and there is enough good in us to fuel progress towards a society in which human potential can be realised.

I am deeply suspicious about the way the Catholic Church in Ireland thinks and acts in matters to do with Britain and I think its anti-British posture may have been a factor in influencing the people to condone the violence.

When I lived in Cork for a few years in the 1970s, I saw people with a strong sense of community. The most difficult part to understand was how these kind, gentle people could allow the brutality of "The Troubles", which has been damaging to everyone, unless it comes from the Catholic Church, which exerted a medieval influence on the people to keep them from the liberating influence of protestant Britain. The official line from the Vatican was that the best way to Catholic emancipation in Ireland was through cooperation with the government. However, a shillelagh has two ends: it might be the heavy end that does the damage, but someone has to be on the handle.

I was friendly with a local man, a practising Catholic, who told me that his priest had encouraged him as a child to believe that the English had horns – quite literally! I frequently pressed him to decide whether an English Catholic would be more evil than an Irish Protestant. He eventually conceded that the English part was worse than the Protestant part. Of course, I was thoroughly bad being both English and Protestant. This betrays the extent to which the Catholic Church triumphed in turning a class struggle into a national and religious conflict.

The Troubles became routine in the minds of people, its dehumanising brutality hidden using that clever Catholic double-think that is evoked whenever the preferred behaviour – in matters such as birth control, abortion, morality, violence – conflicts with Catholic teaching. They know it's going on because they allow it, but they don't think about it. The repugnant part of this is that the violence was unnecessary.

The Act of Union of 1801 brought Ireland into The United Kingdom of Great Britain and Ireland. It was a full and equal member of the nation. From that time and up to the First World War there were movements in Britain and Ireland to improve conditions for the working class. The British Empire was a great success and it did ultimately

6

create the wealth that improved life for all classes, but for the working class only after a measure of democracy had been established and liberal political thought and trade unions had nibbled at the previously unconditional authority of the ruling classes.

There were periodic demonstrations and uprisings. In Ireland there were small scale rebellions and non-violent movements such as the Catholic Emancipation movement, the Repeal Association and the Land League. In Britain we had the Luddite riots, the Peterloo Massacre, the Swing riots and the Tolpuddle Martyrs and protesting workers were imprisoned, hanged, sabre charged and deported. On both islands we had the suffragists' movement and the rise of trade unions.

In some ways the working class in Ireland did better than in Britain. Two laws of 1851 established in Ireland the most comprehensive free medical care available in the British Isles and it would be more than 50 years before it was matched in Britain. This was opposed by the Catholic Church who saw it as promoting socialism and conflicting with the principle of individual responsibility.

It was a liberal Protestant idea that could weaken the Catholic Church's grip on the poor.

By the end of the 19th century, Land Reform had brought owner occupation to nearly half of all Irish holdings. The reforms were driven by socially responsible Catholics and Protestants and Irish society was not, at that time, polarised by religion.

In Britain, papal authority was purged in the sixteenth century. The liberalising effect in Great Britain, stimulated by the famous Protestant work ethic, enabled the industrial revolution and the expansion of the British Empire. In Ireland, Catholicism was allowed to continue as the religion of more than 90% of the population.

Man does have a spiritual dimension and, although science has increasingly helped us to make sense of nature's mysteries, a relationship with God continues to be the choice of many to manage the mysteries within ourselves.

Organised religions offer a convenient one-stop-shop and offer to serve all our needs, nicely packaged – a spiritual supermarket. Having established themselves as the middlemen between man and God they are able to impose rules that ensure they can collect a charge for the necessities.

"You can't lay together until you are joined in holy matrimony; walk this way. A child's immortal soul is in peril until it is christened; pay at the door. You must go to mass at least once a week and tell us all your inner secrets; so we can look for opportunities to strengthen our grip and extract further revenue. You have to be buried in holy ground; otherwise your soul cannot go to heaven."

It's good, steady business that can be kept going if people are denied the freedom to think for themselves.

A side effect in Ireland was that social development was retarded, but that was good for maintaining the status quo and the church maintained its grip on the people. Also the Irish gentry were given the opportunity to shirk their responsibilities, leaving support for the poor to the church that claimed a higher mandate from Rome.

In practice, there was not much support for the poor from the church, the gentry or the government.

Dissent in the United Kingdom, including Ireland, was fostered in the nineteenth century by the laissez-faire attitude of elitist Conservative governments. Free market capitalism had shown its unacceptable face when it waited for economic progress to feed the poor. It did not. The notable example in Ireland was the potato famine, which lasted 7 years from 1845, when nearly a million died and two million emigrated, mostly to America. Conditions for the working class in Britain were also poor and there was an exodus on a similar scale from Britain at this time.

Early in the 20th century, workers in Britain were joining trade unions in order to use collective bargaining to improve their conditions and partially balance the unrestrained power of the merchant and ruling classes. Trade unions spread to Ireland, some progress was made and dockers in Dublin won wage increases. In 1913, Dublin tram workers initiated strike action. The employers locked them out and the winter brought desperate conditions for their families, with the children suffering the most. There was support from British unions who contributed generously to the strike fund and offered to take Dublin children into their members' homes for the duration of the strike. Enter the Catholic Church, who successfully vetoed the offer, declaring that Catholic children would be corrupted in English homes; they preferred to see the children starving than to risk them learning that Englishmen did not, in fact, have horns.

Political progress using constitutional means was being made in Ireland, as intelligent leaders emerged who were negotiating changes and improvements for the working and peasant classes using the influence of the Irish MPs (86 in 1885, for example) in the British Parliament.

However, progress was inhibited, especially when there was a Conservative Government that was concerned about what the precedent Home Rule could set for other parts of the empire. When Gladstone and the Liberals were in power, two Home Rule bills were passed, but enactment was blocked by the Conservative House of Lords who, then, had sufficient powers of veto.

The third Home Rule Bill was passed and put on the Statute Book in 1914, but was suspended when the Kaiser's ambitions precipitated war, to become effective at the end of the conflict (which would be all over by Christmas!) The slowness of the reform process gave opportunity to impatient and unscrupulous men who chose a path of violence. This was established with the Easter Uprising of 1916 and, although this was relatively easily put down, a new direction had been set.

Many Irishmen, both Protestant and Catholic served in the British army during the war, including the majority of the Irish Volunteers; the rebels.

After the war, order continued to break down, especially in Cork and Kerry where the violent campaign of the rebels, who formed the IRA in 1919, was particularly targeted at the police force – The Royal Irish Constabulary. Ex-soldiers and other drafted recruits from Britain supplemented the police after many of its Irish members and their families had been intimidated and murdered. The war had provided military training and experience for both the rebels and the enforcers.

Because of their mish-mash, two tone uniforms, these police reinforcements became known as the Black and Tans. Many of them had returned from the trenches of the Great War to find unemployment in Britain and not the land fit for heroes they had been led to expect.

Disillusioned, some were tempted by the pay - 10 shillings a day plus board and lodging – to go to Ireland where they became an undisciplined force and met the thuggery of the IRA in kind. This was just the worst response for a civilised society; it turned the balance between peaceful evolution and revolution and it confirmed Britain as the enemy of Ireland.

Although provoked by a sustained campaign of brutal assaults on the police, it seems incongruous that as Britain was remembering the horror and waste of the Great War, which it justified only by a belief in a righteous fight to preserve freedom (The Great War for Civilisation), it was giving little thought to the way in which the Irish uprising was being put down in Dublin, Cork and Kerry. The Irish were misguided; the British inept.

The hostility between Catholics and Protestants in Ireland is not doctrinal, but was generated by a reaction to modernisation by the Pope and his team. It was exacerbated by Irish Protestantism, which took on some of the dogmatic and inflexible nature of Irish Catholicism as people became divided and competed for different political ideals.

There was revolution, in the futile hope that independence would solve the problems. Manifestly it did not and the Irish would surely have progressed faster to a better quality of life and opportunity if they could have been patient enough to allow the social progress that was coming to carry them to a peaceful, independent and united future.

The Irish didn't seem to realise that the lot of the working classes in England in the 19th and early 20th centuries was little better than that of those in Ireland. Their struggle should have been for working class emancipation with their brothers in England and not against the British. Surely we would all now be stronger, richer and less scarred if we had continued to share our histories.

In 1884, the electorate of The United Kingdom extended only to men owning property. Women paying rates were added in 1907 and the vote was extended to all men over 21 and women over 30 in 1918. It was not until 1928 that all adults over 21 were able to participate in the democratic process – the United Kingdom was not a democracy until well after the First World War. As the electorate became more representative and the influence of the working class, women and younger people started to have an effect, more egalitarian policies were demanded and socially sensitive policies began to improve conditions for working people. The Irish would certainly have been able to choose their future through the ballot box.

A few British army regiments, including the Wiltshires with whom my grandfather had enlisted, were sent to Ireland to help keep the peace. Born in 1900, he had just missed active service in the Great War and would have been 20-years-old. The terms of his father's will obliged him to wait until his 26th birthday for his inheritance. His father had also instructed that his sons should see military service, presumably to aid their personal development.

Although not well educated, my grandfather was healthy, handsome and had tales of property in England; enough to appeal to a colleen desperate for a better life than that available to her in Ireland in the 1920's.

Fraternising with British soldiers was discouraged in the Irish community and this was not an easy courtship for the young couple.

When my grandfather returned to England, my grandmother followed him and they were married in 1923 in Christchurch, a small coastal town on the western edge of The New Forest.

I find it difficult to imagine what my grandmother's character might have been or how she had been affected by the troubled times. She had a lot of bad luck: growing up at the worst time in Irish history, choosing a husband who turned out to be unsupportive, and falling into poor health. There was little space for tenderness and it is not surprising that my mother and her siblings had hard childhoods. She found support from her religion in the later part of her life and my aunts and my mother remembered her as a good Catholic imposing discipline and character on her children.

My grandparents started their married life together and a baby boy arrived on Christmas day, 1923. My grandfather was now working as a bricklayer's labourer but he would come into his inheritance in three years and my grandmother was looking forward to a better life.

They had a second son in 1925 but he died in 1926, the year the inheritance was released. The young family moved on to their inherited farm and my mother was born the following year.

Photographs show them well dressed and my grandmother must have still been optimistic about the future. Their holding was only a few acres, but my grandfather also bought a lorry and obtained an income from haulage work.

Six more children, five of whom survived, were born over the next ten years but my grandfather showed little interest in the family. Their fortunes declined, the property was lost and the family moved first into a rented house in the outskirts of Christchurch, then to a small terraced house in the same area.

My grandmother's health declined after a heart attack and my mother, as the oldest girl, took on domestic duties that increased as she grew older. She seems to have accepted her role and I don't remember her speaking negatively about it or about her mother.

Children at this time in working class families were generally expected to make a contribution to work in the home. This was only a generation after the Education Reform Bill of 1893, under which children under 13-years-old were no longer to be treated as economic production units.

Country families are often close and, in this family, there was some support in difficult times. However, my grandfather's mother did not seem to be able to help when my grandmother was hospitalised following her heart attack and her seven children had to be farmed out to relations and willing families in the community (this was the welfare system in rural Hampshire at the time), two of the children were sent to her for care. She started to make plans to send them and the other children to the Cottage Homes in Christchurch. This was the local orphanage and the children would be put up for adoption if this became more than a temporary arrangement. She may have believed this could give them a better future and, now at 60-years-old, she may also have felt she had done her share of bringing up children, and may not have had the stamina or the inclination to take responsibility for her son's children.

My grandmother was obliged to discharge herself from hospital and return home to do her best to care for her children. She never recovered her health and died 14 years later at the age of 51. The amount of support she received from her husband and his family must have been a disappointment.

As I look at this history, with the detachment of a generation, I see my mother's childhood with few of the experiences most of us cherish. The children of the family all experienced a poor childhood but my mother, as the oldest girl, probably carried the larger part of the burden until she left home. It was then the turn of her sister, two years younger, to help their mother, and all the children were expected to do their bit.

Those who knew my mother were impressed by her character, resilience and work ethic. Where did this strength come from? Is it carried in the genes waiting to be activated when the right circumstances prevail? Certainly she learned resilience and developed a capacity for hard work during her childhood but there was much more to my mother than just that.

War broke out again in 1939, but at first had little effect on rural Hampshire. German bombers were seen from May 1940, many passing over, but some targeting Bournemouth and Christchurch.

My mother's education was interrupted by time in hospital and in convalescence with rheumatic fever. Also half-day schooling had been imposed so evacuees could share the school facilities. She left school on her fourteenth birthday and started work in a boarding house near Christchurch Quay where Canadian servicemen were lodged. Her wages were a small contribution to the family income. The work and the treatment of her employer were demeaning and she escaped this by finding herself alternative work with Lovage the Baker in Christchurch where she was now treated well and had happy memories of this period.

Later she found work as a maid at the Avon Royal Hotel in Bournemouth, popular with wealthy Jews. Bournemouth had developed on its reputation of mild climate and healthy sea air and it could be reached from London relatively easily by rail or, for those able to afford the luxury, by car.

This particular hotel was favoured by the Jewish community. I suppose I first heard about my mother's early life was when I was a child and the way she described the clientele as "wealthy Jews" led me to suppose that all Jews were wealthy and, perhaps, that all wealthy people were Jews.

Beyond this association with money, I had no idea what a Jew was; such is the way information about the outside world is slowly assimilated by a boy in a quiet country community.

She was giving her wages to her mother but had now learned how to earn good tips, which she was able to keep for herself and she was able to buy new clothes for the first time.

When the hotel needed a new waitress my mother successfully applied for the position and managed to negotiate a pay increase. After gaining some experience and hoping to escape from an unhappy home, she found herself live-in jobs further afield, first in London with a family she had met at the Avon Royal and later in a hotel in Kent. However, it was only a few months before she was drawn back to the Christchurch area and she obtained a live-in position in The Kings Arms in Christchurch where she worked until the end of the war.

My mother wrote down her memories of her early life. These writings were in the form of a hand written manuscript which I found humbling to read. I think it was written in 1981 and was on the back of old Hampshire

County Library forms. If Mum was true to form, she would have salvaged the paper when the forms were out of date. In writing down her memories perhaps she was trying to put her life in perspective and manage her bereavement as she struggled to come to terms with losing my father who had died in 1977. She added to her writings over the years and I only became aware of some of them after her death.

My mother was never negative about her past or critical of her parents to me. I think she chose to soften the reality of a very hard start in life in order to be able to be positive about building an adult life for herself.

Thirty one years later, after my father died, she started building again: a widow's life this time. She joined societies, gave talks on New Forest life and made new friends; an active and useful member of the community warmly remembered by those friends.

Chapter 3

Wars and Peace

"'Monte Carlo' the super Ice Show appearing twice nightly at Westover Ice Rink is easily proving one of Bournemouth's greatest summer attractions. George Morley and Dorothy Paddock are the perfect pair in grace and rhythm and their acrobatic speciality is one of the important features of the show." This was the report in the Bournemouth Times of 25 August 1939.

George Morley, my father, was especially athletic and had discovered a talent for figure skating that took him to the top of a profession that had been popular in the 1920s and 30s and even sustained him in a show business lifestyle during the depression of 1932. His social acquaintances had been the well-known actors and sportsmen of the day. Included among them were James Robertson Justice, David Niven - who was starting to enjoy a successful film career in Hollywood - and Primo Carnero, the only man to have been the world champion in both heavyweight boxing and wrestling.

Dad told me he had chatted up an attractive Italian girl in a bar in Richmond and had felt he was doing well when Carnero came in and claimed back his girlfriend. A risky choice Dad had thought, but the Italian giant was off duty and a tactical retreat saved any discomfort.

At £5.10s a week, his pay in 1939 was more than three times the average wage. At that time the Football League imposed a maximum wage for the playing season of £8 a week. Dad's wage was not a fortune but sufficient for a young man to be able to afford some luxuries.

He drove a Mercedes sports car and I remember him telling me he could get from Grosvenor House in London to the Westover in Bournemouth in 2 hours 15 minutes; quite some going on pre-war roads and even allowing for a bit of selective memory.

Before the war, ice spectaculars were a favourite entertainment and my father was one of the stars. He and his older sister, Lily, had many successes in competitions and performed exhibitions together and with other partners. My father starred in some of the successful shows of the period with such titles as *Prince of Voravia* and *Monte Carlo*. He skated first in London at the Stoll Theatre on Kingsway and, later, at Southampton Ice Rink and Westover Ice Club in Bournemouth.

The Grosvenor House Hotel on Park Lane in London has a famous feature: The Great Room, capable of accommodating 2000 diners under lavish glass chandeliers and is claimed to be the largest ballroom in Europe. Before the war, this room was an ice rink where society people went to skate. My father was the resident professional there for a while and taught many to skate, including the princesses Elizabeth and Margaret.

In 1932, my father married his skating partner, Eva Steven and they had a son, Michael, in 1934.

Lily had also married in 1932 to a wealthy Irishman, Gawin Downes-Martin, living in Christchurch. My father and Gawin had become friends and my father had crewed Gawin's yacht from time to time; they were part of the jet-set of the day and Gawin was a genuine adventurer-playboy, fond of fast cars, expensive boats and aeroplanes. I have a photograph of Lily and Gawin going off on their honeymoon in Gawin's Klemm two-seater bi-plane.

This seems to have been the era of the wealthy thrill seeker. There were reports in the local papers of Gawin's reckless adventures and failed treasure hunting expeditions and of other adventurers: Malcolm Campbell, "the first

18

person to drive an automobile at over 300mph" on the Bonneville Salt Flats; Squadron-leader F.R.D. Swain, "flew higher than man has ever flown"; Captain Stanley Halse, "ahead in the Portsmouth-Johannesburg Air Race'; Downes-Martin, "has thrilled Christchurch on more than one occasion and his name became associated with dare devil escapades".

In July1936, the Spanish Civil War broke out when the right wing Spanish Army generals representing the National Front started their (eventually) successful bid to take power from the socialist Popular Front (republican) government that had been democratically elected but had only a tenuous grip on power. Part of the government's manifesto had been to roll back the influence of the Catholic Church. The clerics aligned with the National Front and again, as in the Irish situation, the clerics preferred violent revolution to erosion of their influence.

Volunteers from Britain and other countries, to become known as the International Brigade, joined the fighting on the republican side. Some, like George Orwell, were motivated by ideology; others were paid mercenaries and a few, like Gawin, just thought it would be fun. He offered his flying skills, was accepted and became a member of the International Brigade's fliers they called "The Suicide Squad", because of their lack of preparation and obsolete aircraft that would go against the Heinkels and Fiats piloted by well trained regular airmen. Gawin took a fatal bullet to the head on his first sortie.

The Daily Express of 30 September 1936 reported Lily as saying: "All the four years we have been married I have known he would die violently like this. He seemed to be stretching his luck to its limit all his life. If he was not flying then he would be motor boat racing, or speeding some other way."

She added: "He went to London for a weekend five weeks ago, came back breathless and hurriedly packed up a few things. Said he was going to Spain, did I mind? I knew there was nothing I could say."

And she finished with: "He knew nothing of fighting but that did not worry him. He was just fed up with hanging about the house with nothing to do. He has never had a job, always had enough money and that bored him sometimes."

Lily always appeared to have money, but not as much as Gawin's lifestyle would have suggested. In fact she inherited Gawin's estate of £305-2s-9d (about £10,000 in today's money), so his money had all but run out and the war adventure, perhaps, offered some sort of final fling.

Unfortunately, like many show business marriages, my dad's failed when Eva ran off with another skater, a Czech named Otto Gold, to live in Canada, leaving my father with Michael. This was around 1938. Eva was divorced, the decree nisi being granted on 30 October 1939 on the grounds of her adultery with Otto.

There was support from the family, in particular, Lily and my father's parents who looked after Michael from this time on. I think he was well cared for and Lily sent him to an independent school.

It seems that Lily had hoped that my father and Michael would live with her, but Dad declined. He later confided that this arrangement would have had all the disadvantages of marriage and none of its pleasures!

Sadly, the relationship between brother and sister that had been close became strained. Perhaps Lily had become too used to having her own way, or perhaps it was just the circumstances.

My father had come from modest beginnings, growing up in the Cheetham Hill area of Manchester. He had only a basic education and he left school at 14 with only a First Class Certificate for Swimming. When I was a child he relayed to me stories of running street battles he had in the 1920s with boys from the Jewish community. This was the second time I had heard about Jews and I had not heard reference to any other racial or ethnic group at that point in my life.

This would have been before the Windrush brought the first West Indians to help fill the need for labour in Britain's expanding economy of the 1950s and long before Commonwealth citizens from the sub-continent began to take up their entitlement to reside here. I suppose Jews were the first immigrant group to maintain a separate culture within British society.

There seemed to be a slight negative connotation in these references to Jews. This is probably how prejudice, even if not strong, is passed on in families and communities. It is, perhaps, to strengthen our tribal allegiance and put us on guard against others who might threaten us.

It is easier now, in a more modern Britain, to see the benefits and stimulation that people with different ideas can bring, but it has been worrying, threatening perhaps, for people to see foreigners displacing parts of the native population. It is most threatening for those lower down the class system and those with little education. We can gain more than we lose from the diversity of a multi-cultural society, but there will probably always be tensions that we have to manage.

The swimming certificates and class photographs that survive differentiate his city upbringing from my mother's rural and small town situation. There was just a little more opportunity in Britain's third city than in Hampshire's rural backwater.

My dad's father, William George Henry Morley, had been a postal clerk and had made a little progress in his career before the First World War broke out. He had volunteered immediately and served until 1919. His service was rewarded with the usual medals: the 1914-15 Star, The War Medal and The Victory Medal. He also received the French Croix de Guerre, which was awarded to non-French troops who were mentioned in despatches, but I have not been able to find more information on this. He and his contemporaries were known as the "Old Contemptibles" – the name the veterans gave themselves after the war, remembering (supposedly) that the Kaiser had called them, in exasperation, a "contemptible little army" when they held up his troops so effectively in 1914.

He survived the war, but "The Old Man", as they then called him, suffered effects of gas attacks and shell shock for the rest of his life. The man who came back from the war was a different person to the one who had gone four and a half years earlier.

After the war he was unable to resume his Post Office career and was retired with a modest pension and a small lump sum, which he used to start an electrical business. He seems to have been a capable engineer and I remember the machines he made from scratch in his home workshop, but he was not a businessman.

The business was a company that carried out electrical installations. Many, perhaps most, of his customers were from the Jewish community. It seems they had been successful enough to be able to afford to have electric lighting installed in their homes and synagogues.

The family has it that they were less successful at paying their bills. The Old Man was casual about collecting his money and eventually was overwhelmed by bad debts. It is probable that the failure of his business was mainly due to lack of business acumen, perhaps exacerbated by the effects on his temperament of his war experience. However, if you are going to blame someone else, Jews painted into the role of scapegoat over the generations, are good candidates.

The Old Man retired from the business without money and, with my grandmother, moved from Manchester to live with my father in Christchurch. At first they lived on Dad's houseboat, but later were able to move into a thatched cottage in Godwinscroft on the edge of the New Forest.

Dad had learned to skate at the Ice Palace – England's first ice rink – in Manchester and had become proficient enough to be able to make this his profession. He had left school at 14 to work for his father, but had not enjoyed crawling about under synagogue floors pulling heavy rubber cables. The skating was a happy release and an escape route. He left home to go to London at the age of 17.

He had an aunt, whose name was Fanny Henrietta, but she was known as Susan. Susan lived with the family for a while but eventually secured a good job as manageress of the Singer Sewing Machine Company's franchise in Manchester. She was more successful in business than her brother and made a good living. She moved into her own accommodation, a flat over a sewing machine shop and Dad had happy memories of holidays in North Wales, hosted by Susan and her friend, Dolly. Susan and Dolly were emancipated young women and mobile.

They travelled around on Dolly's motorcycle combination and must have raised eyebrows at the time, when women were expected to have husbands and behave discretely and just a couple of years before women over the age of 30 would win the vote.

When Dad left for London, it was Susan who bought him his first suit and put money in his pocket to get him started.

My grandfather became somewhat eccentric. He thought he could improve his health by connecting himself to an electric source – one pole to his toe and the other to a metal comb with which he combed his hair. He talked about his ridiculous ideas; such suggestions as harnessing power from the tides to generate electricity. He relieved his frustration at not being understood in several ways. One was in the privy at the bottom of the garden, overlooking open fields, where he kept a shotgun so he could shoot the pigeons that flew over, while he contemplated on his whitewashed wooden seat. I remember him as granddads

23

should be – a little bad tempered and having a big white beard.

The Old Man died in 1952 in Boscombe Hospital. My dad later told me two stories about this.

During one visit The Old Man had implored Dad to "nip out and get him a pint". He was very ill with the later stages of cancer at the time. Dad nipped out and, on his return, was told, "You drink it for me; I've got no stomach left, but I'll watch you – and make sure you enjoy it."

Very near the end, The Old Man said to Dad, "See that name on the bed?" (Beds were often donated by patients). It was Solly Fisher.

"Look, I'm haunted by Jews, even at the end."

He died that night. I don't believe he really blamed them for the failure of his business, but he may have felt some irony that his last days were attended by Jewish charity.

If there was any animosity here my dad didn't inherit it: he always displayed fairness towards everyone he dealt with.

My great-grandfather was William George Morley. He too had done military service for his country having joined the Royal Navy in 1850 as "Boy First Class". He sailed in ships not much more advanced that those of the Tudor navy; he went to the Baltic and Crimean wars in a wooden ship, HMS Stromboli, clad with copper and powered by sail and paddle wheels driven by primitive steam engines. The ship's company consisted of 112 sailors, 20 marines and 24 boys and they fought in the Baltic, Sebastopol and Azoff. He transferred to the HMS Furious, a similar ship, which took him to China where he saw engagement at Taku Forts and Canton as the British stamped their authority on their empire. Other vessels took him to Australia and the Caribbean during his ten years' service.

He came out of the navy with good references and joined the police force where he did well as a detective for a time, but was eventually discharged for drunkenness on duty. He became a prison warder and met a good woman who seems to have pulled him together. In middle age they had two children: my grandfather and the wonderful Susan.

Here is an example of a family story having developed over time. It was said that my grandfather, WGH, had been born in Strangeways Prison in Manchester where his father, WG, had been Prison Governor. My father's sister Gwen, a somewhat eccentric but very likeable aunt, remembered his funeral as one in which he was borne to the cemetery on a gun carriage - full military honours. When I investigated Home Office census and birth records, I discovered that WGH was not born in Strangeways but Devizes Prison, when WG was serving as a night watchman, not Governor. The gun carriage funeral was presumably a coincident funeral of a senior officer and not that of a Yeoman of ten years' service in the ranks.

I never understood why my dad's sisters had such a compulsion to talk up their humble working class origins. They did all advance to respectable middle class lives; Gwen through hard work and business acumen, Connie through marrying a hardworking and moderately successful engineer and Lily through marriage.

We are not at all a military family, but each generation before me has served our country when the need arose. I think they have done this, certainly in the two world wars, to safeguard our liberal democracy and the values that have been established.

Dad was the fifth of six children; three boys and three girls. The oldest, Eric, followed his father into the post office where he worked for 58 years until the age of 72, although he did have a 6 year sabbatical from 1939 to 1945. I inherited his medals; four from the war and the Empire Service Medal for his first 50 years as a postman. He was my Godfather; our relationship was warm but contact was rare due to distance and finances.

Then came Connie, who stayed in Manchester and married a local man, Len Buckley. Len had been an apprentice at the Lancashire Dynamo Company and worked his way up to become the Works Manager. Connie and Len lived comfortably in the Manchester suburbs where they brought up their two children, Maureen and John. I have always got on well with John and we have kept in contact over the years.

Gwen was the next. She joined the skating scene and met an ice hockey player, Archie Stinchcombe whom she married. They worked hard all their lives building up and running their sports' business in Nottingham where Archie had been the coach of the Nottingham Panthers' ice hockey team. His credentials for this job were his participation, in 1936 and captaincy in 1948, of the British Olympic team.

Uncle Archie won the gold medal in the 1936 Olympics and received it from one Adolf Hitler. He was quick enough to ask Adolf for his autograph and this was given, signed on the edge of his player's pass.

Diaries purportedly written by Hitler and published in 1983 were investigated. Initially, handwriting experts compared them with letters by Hitler and declared them to be genuine, but it emerged that the letters were by the same forger. Uncle Archie's pass was used as a genuine example of the Hitler hand in the investigation that exposed the hoax.

Lily was the fourth child of the family. She had two more husbands after Gawin Downes-Martin. First, there was a wealthy businessman from Bournemouth named Beechy Newman, whom she married just before the war and divorced when he failed to pay her sufficient attention. Then there was Air Commodore Ric Richardson, with whom she lived on the Isle of Wight until his death in old age in the 1960s.

Harry was the youngest member of the family. He also served in the RAF in the Second World War. He lived a decent life in Southampton and brought up three children. There was only occasional contact with this branch of the family.

I always accepted that my father came from a Lancashire family; he and his brothers and sisters were born and grew up in Manchester. However, through researching the family history I have found out that the Morleys came from Hampshire and the Isle of Wight for at least three generations before my father. With my mother's genealogy, this gives me a pretty strong Hampshire pedigree. I don't remember Dad speaking fondly or romantically about the North the way some northerners do. Perhaps it takes several generations to absorb a real feeling and affection for a place and its culture.

My father was under contract for the ice show *Monte Carlo* at the Westover from April to October 1939. Neville Chamberlin declared war on Germany at 11:00 am on 3 September 1939. Leisure activities including bowls, football and dancing were cancelled by government order on the 8 September and, on 13 September, my father had enlisted for army service. He did not complete his skating contract.

Dad had a pretty eventful army career. He was enlisted to the Territorial Army and assigned to division 88DR (Despatch Rider) of the Royal Army Signals Corps and posted, initially, to 42nd Division Army Signals. He embarked on the British Expeditionary Force (BEF) on 11 April 1940. His division was evacuated from Dunkirk on 8 June, but he was not with them. My grandmother received the communication on Army Form B. 104—83 that thousands of mothers and wives must have received at that time: "Madam, I regret to inform you that a report has been received from the War Office to the effect that (No.) 2588587 (Rank) Signalman (Name) Morley G.F., (Regiment) ROYAL CORPS OF SIGNALS posted as 'missing' on 14 June 1940."

As a DR, he would have been moving between army units and he had been behind enemy lines when the evacuation took place. He was left behind but fared better than the thousands of foot soldiers who were slaughtered on the beaches. He eventually found his way to the coast and looked for a way to get home. At the age of 28 he was more mature than many of the other soldiers and may have been more resourceful than most. He picked up a couple of young soldiers who were confused and in need of support. After some foraging and, while avoiding the enemy, he found a rowing dinghy and thought their best chance would be to simply row home.

They set off after dark in what they thought was the right direction. Daylight came and they continued until they spotted a warship coming towards them. At first they could not tell whether it was British or German. It was British; they were taken on board and returned to Southampton.

In Southampton his only thought was to get home and have a bath. After weeks of sleeping rough he was dirty and had unwanted guests about his person. He "found" an army motorbike unattended in the docks and borrowed it. After passing the security post at the gate at speed, he kept going through Southampton and to the New Forest. "Home" was the thatched cob cottage in Godwinscroft, just outside Christchurch – a rather different situation to the beaches of Normandy.

Although he had been missing in action for only a matter of weeks, on his arrival, he discovered that his mother and Lily had discarded his belongings and clothes. After a bath he managed to find something to wear, borrowed from neighbours. He gave himself two weeks leave before travelling to Catterick by train to find his unit. On arrival, his commanding officer (CO) felt he would need some rest and immediately sent him home on two weeks' disembarkation leave.

There was a letter my dad kept, dated 26 Jan 1945, from L/Cpl. Hugh M. Pert 7621303 REME 812 Armd. TPS Workshop BLA, thanking him for "all he did for him", but with no detail. Could this have been one of the young soldiers he brought back from Dunkirk?

Dad's official army record shows movements of his army division but not of all his personal activities. For example, it does not record his assignment to the 8th Army in North Africa where he carried messages for General Montgomery. That would have been around October 1942. I am sure he was there from the stories he told me and he was awarded the Africa Star (required 28 days in that action to qualify), which I now have.

For the next months, he was on "home" service (based in England), with occasional leave. On one such break, not long after his service in North Africa, he visited Manchester and dropped in on old friends. He had always been fond of animals and, as a boy, had spend much of his time in Manchester's Tib Street where all sorts of animals were traded as pets and he may have paid it a nostalgic visit.

He had enjoyed having sisters or, perhaps, he made having sisters tolerable by playing brotherly jokes on them and he seems to have managed to keep his sense of humour through much of the war. During the Manchester visit he called to see his sister, Connie, in her comfortable home in Sale. Connie had always been the most vulnerable of his sisters and, now that she felt very middle class, would definitely be fair game. Adulthood was no reason not to play the now well tried role; it just meant the game needed to be a little more subtle.

By the time he got to Connie's he had a monkey on his shoulder. She was used to his jokes and, on this occasion, she was determined not to be flustered by him.

"Would you like a cup of tea George and what would the monkey like?" she enquired in her calmest voice.

29

"Thanks Connie, I'd love one. The monkey likes boiled eggs," was the nonchalant reply.

Without fuss, an egg was boiled and offered to the monkey who took it, examined it and peeled it dexterously. The egg was sniffed and examined again, then, with distain, hurled at Connie. It split and emptied its yolk down the front of her dress.

"He likes them hard boiled; I should have said." There was mock apology in his voice.

Dad and the monkey left, satisfied. Well, she didn't manage not to be flustered. Dad went back to his duties and the monkey...

When Connie's son, John, relayed this story to me in recent times, he said his mother had thought that Dad had brought the monkey back from Africa, but I don't remember this from Dad's telling of the story and I think it more likely that he borrowed it from an old acquaintance in Tib Street.

During the next year or so Dad carried despatches around England until he went back to France on 14 June 1944. The D-Day landings had begun on 6 June. He served in that arena and was part of the British Army on the Rhine (BAOR). His memorabilia include many photographs of Germany, including Berlin.

I heard about some of the hazards Dad experienced. The enemy would try to stop the free movement of DRs. On some regular routes, patrolled by the Luftwaffe, crossing open country needed careful attention to the sky. Other places had snipers lying in wait and, on one occasion, an officer he was giving a lift to was shot dead on the pillion of his bike. Another time, a cheese wire stretched across the road took him off the bike but had, luckily, struck the flask that he carried strapped to his chest and he didn't suffer serious injury. Others had been decapitated by these devices.

He was captured once and put into a field prisoner of war camp, but it doesn't sound as though the Germans were all that determined to keep him. He slipped under the wire at night and rejoined his unit.

A clever trick he told me about was his way of finding his motorcycle in the dark on the occasions when he left it in a wood; to make a reconnaissance on foot behind enemy lines. He would gather a handful of glow worms, plentiful in France in the summer and place them in his headlamp. This would guide him back to the machine as long as he was in the right area.

In the last days of the war he was travelling by jeep and came across a platoon of German soldiers. They surrendered to him and he marched them back to his unit expecting a commendation. The CO was furious at his stupidity.

"How do you think we are going to feed them and where will they be billeted?"

In April 1945, he was one of the first Allied soldiers to reach Belsen and witness the unspeakable horror of that place with its emaciated survivors. He told me he had simply not known how to relate to these people, people who were no longer relating to anything. He offered cigarettes to a couple of men; they ate the cigarettes.

Dad was demobilised from the army 29 December 1945 with a suit and a gratuity of £60. He borrowed some money from his sister Lily and bought an Armstrong Siddley to be used as a taxi. The taxi drivers, who had established their business while Dad was at war, closed ranks (literally) and squeezed him out of the business.

Chapter 4

Be Poor in a Nice Place

George Morley met Molly Westridge in the Kings Arms bar in Christchurch. She was the barmaid he chatted up and cajoled into calling him when a customer needed a taxi. Their relationship grew. Two people in need of soul mates, they became close and soon realised they could share a dream of building a decent future.

It was very difficult for the returning troops on demobilisation to find work if they were not returning to a secure position. My parents were fortunate to be offered a position as a married couple, running a hotel in Jersey that was owned by an army officer under whom my father had served. They planned to marry but my grandparents refused permission. They were able to do this with a 19-year-old at that time. Mum went to court to seek permission to marry. Her parents opposed, citing my father's age (he was then 34) and his status as a divorcee, but omitted to give credit for his six years' war service and good character.

However, the magistrate had also been headmaster of my mother's secondary school and he knew the family situation. Permission was given and they married. It does not appear in the report of the case but, by the time they were in court, my mother was two months pregnant. The job in Jersey was for a working couple and was no longer feasible. The road ahead would not be easy.

The war was over but celebrations had been brief. Many would have to come to terms with the physical and mental effects of their experience of the conflict. Many more were carrying on with their lives having all but forgotten it ever happened. Looking back at the local newspaper, The Christchurch Times, of that year you see only the briefest references to the war.

Even the victory celebration on the anniversary of peace is low key, done more for appearances than out of any sense of gratitude or recognition.

All that was needed for those who had not been directly affected by the war was to roll the memory of those damaged by this conflict into the small, convenient package of time; two minutes, which had been allocated when Lutyen's memorial obelisk had been commissioned by Lloyd George in 1919. This did the job nicely; they could demonstrate recognition without too much inconvenience, but for those carrying the scars it just reminded them how completely they had been forgotten for the other 525,598 minutes of the year.

Those men and women who had served would remember in silence and few would tell their stories. I have the medals given to my father and his brother, my Godfather. I have stories of the lighter moments and a few of the more poignant ones, told to me by my father over the thirty years that I knew him.

Most of our troops during the Second World War were volunteers and conscripts, not professional soldiers. They served to defend the freedoms they believed in and valued. After the war, the euphoria of victory was short lived and quickly dissolved when the reality of no jobs, no housing and inadequate support became apparent and echoed the situation after The Great War when the promised "land fit for heroes" had not been realised. On 26 July 1945, the Prime Minister who had led us to victory, Winston Churchill, and a complacent Tory party were surprised and voted out in a wave of mass dissatisfaction with the poor prospects that people saw for the economy.

Molly Westridge had become Molly Morley. She had been given no childhood and now she took the opportunity to be with a good man who would give her affection and respect.

My father had been an embarrassment to his sister who had married into a moneyed existence and had jumped into another class, forgetting her roots. He was no longer the successful professional skater but a divorced and penniless ex-serviceman; no proper job, no viable trade or profession and no prospects. He had a new wife from a working class family and she was expecting a baby. Marrying my mother was the last straw for Lily and her relationship with Dad broke down completely. He sold the taxi, repaid her loan and went north.

Such success as I achieved, which has been moderately satisfying considering my beginnings and family traditions, was due to the example and expectations of my parents; not spoken or demanded, but inspired by their desire to establish a platform in life and modest success without extreme want or hunger and with security.

That my mother loved me I have no doubt; that she inspired me, subtly, lovingly, I have no doubt. She chose to ignore the imperfections and to celebrate the achievements. I was her vicarious success, the next step on the ladder she had worked so hard to make possible.

I think she was at peace by the time she died, having dealt with the challenges of her life and experienced enough joy to feel that the effort and constancy had been rewarded.

I was born six months after the wedding. I think this was an embarrassment to my mother and she never spoke of it; it was a digression in a time in which such things were shameful. Not during my childhood, not during my adolescence, not during the rest of her life was it mentioned.

Wedding anniversaries were cloaked in just a little obscurity, such that I realised, at some point, that I may have been conceived out of wedlock. It didn't worry me that this may have happened; I had the full amount of love and support that anyone could wish from their parents, but

35

it bothered me a little that it bothered my mother enough to not talk about it. It was a skeleton in the closet but it only rattled a little and only once a year. I wonder if it would have affected her feelings about this if she had known, as we can see now from the genealogical record that it had happened regularly in many generations of both sides of my family and many other families.

One person offered friendship and support; Dad's aunt, Susan. Warm, generous and human, she had always been willing to help those less fortunate than herself and now she offered her nephew space in her home in Hazel Grove, Stockport. Perhaps there would be work in The North? To move away from The New Forest was a daunting prospect for Mum. Although she might have had reason to want to distance herself from her family she seemed, nonetheless, to have valued the idea of family relationships and she had put a lot of effort into her family throughout her childhood. Also, she was strongly attracted, even anchored, to The Forest; it was a part of her and she a part of it. She loved it in all its seasons and her conversation was usually punctuated by references to what was happening in it; in the late summer when the heather bloomed on the broad, open heathlands, anytime when a sunny period brought the gorse into its sunshine yellow, the autumn when wild mushrooms could be gathered from the green areas, the winter when the bare, purple branches were there to break the skyline and the spring when the fresh, new foliage signalled long days again.

But they somehow had to find a way to earn a living, to earn respectability and to build a life. Dad did find work but just temporary jobs labouring and driving.

When the time came to deliver the baby there was no room at the hospital in Stockport and my mother had to go to Macclesfield, 12 miles away. This meant more expense and very few visits, with roads made difficult by the snow and they had no transport. The only way for Dad to get to the hospital was to walk and walk he did. This would be the coldest winter on record and Dad would need to use all his tenacity and resourcefulness to keep his family fed and warm.

Mum was in that hospital from 18 - 30 December 1946. The National Health Service had not yet been established, so there was a bill to pay; £6, less the deposit of £3 that had been paid on entry. The average wage at this time was under £5 a week for a man in skilled employment.

Susan's husband, Jim, maintained the car belonging to Mr. Hazeldene the butcher as a part time job and was able to borrow it to bring us home from Macclesfield.

One of my mother's handwritten manuscripts is called *My Son*. Here are some extracts that give an impression of how she experienced going north.

"This was a big adventure for me as in all my life I had never travelled further north than Basingstoke in Hampshire. I was nineteen-years-old. Susan and Jim lived in a semi-detached house in Hazel grove, Stockport, Cheshire. Susan's husband, Jim, was twenty years younger than herself. You would never have thought so as he looked older, being bald and slightly round shouldered. They welcomed me to their home. They were kindness itself and we became lifelong friends.

Although we found things were no better there as far as employment and housing were concerned. But at least we had a roof over our heads.

This then was the place where I was to spend the greater part of my pregnancy and prepare for the birth of my child.

In 1946, antenatal treatment was not like it is today so the local doctor decided to send me to Macclesfield hospital, some twenty miles away as the nearest local hospital, Stepping Hill was full. In 1946 with the men returning from the war there were a large number of births all over the country. At first I went to Macclesfield hospital

37

once a month. In the later stages it was once in three weeks and the last month, once every week. You didn't consult the doctor at the hospital any more than you had to as you had to pay for consultations and we didn't have any money to spare.

It started to snow heavily early in December and it was bitterly cold. Half the time there was no coal for the fire and, of course, only one room was heated. Then, early on the 18th December 1946 I started my baby. George was sent for and so was Jim. Jim was ever so good. Somehow he conjured up a car and I was rushed to Westpark Hospital, Macclesfield for the birth.

We only had the bare necessities of clothing for the baby as everything was rationed. Then, at 8:05 pm in the evening, this beautiful baby was born. 8lbs 4ozs; a lovely little boy. George was overjoyed at having a son. He was only able to come to the hospital once. I was in there about fourteen days, all over Christmas. The sight of the nurses with lanterns in their red cloaks, going round the wards singing Silent Night was very memorable. It started to snow really hard. There were 17 foot drifts up in those Cheshire hills. All roads were blocked. No buses, so no one came to visit. Fortunately for me I was in a small ward with three other ladies. Their husbands were all farmers and lived nearby. They managed to get through on a farm tractor. They brought us eggs, milk, cheese and butter and other goodies. I suspect they brought some for the nurses as well. The ladies shared all these delights with me.

The nurses took the eggs and cooked them for us. As we were paying daily for our hospital bed, everyone was worried about getting out on time. Eventually, a snow plough broke through. They said it was the worst winter on record. Even the ink in the bottles was frozen. On the way home we had to register the birth in Macclesfield. In these conditions we knew we would not go to Macclesfield again in a hurry. So, on the way home we stopped at the

Registrar's office. I had called the baby Peter Richard.
When George got to the office, he changed it to Peter
George. "

My father was disappointed and angry at the situation he
found himself in after what he considered to be six years
loyal army service. There were a few good people like
Susan and Jim who were supportive, there were ex-
servicemen and women who understood and empathised
and many who had avoided service and now jealously
guarded their jobs. Dad had experienced this with
established taxi drivers in Christchurch. He may have
hoped people in his native Lancashire would have been
more helpful, but this is not what he found. There was little
to go round and generosity generally stretched no further
than family units. For a while he lived in a hostel and
worked in a coal mine some distance away, but those
established in the trade had first call on work at the coal
face where the wages were reasonable.

Dad managed to find a job driving a crane for a company
on the Macclesfield Road, making prefabs; the
prefabricated buildings that were hurriedly conceived and
built to relieve the housing shortage. They had a 10 year
design life but many lasted 50 years and a few are still
giving good service 60 years later.

I remember an old rubber kneeling mat that my mother
kept for many years, long after it was worn out and there
was a story to it that she eventually told me.

A stack of prefabricated building sides at the prefab
works had fallen onto a man who was then trapped and in a
very desperate situation. There was no time to get a crane
and this might have exacerbated the situation anyway. My
father was a big man and very strong, with the ability to
somehow call up reserves of strength. He lifted the
building parts sufficiently for others to pull the man clear.
The man had no money and no way of showing his

gratitude for what he considered was an act that saved his life. He visited Mum and gave her the best thing he owned; a rubber kneeling mat.

My father would feed his family. There was scavenging and recycling to pull together enough basic equipment, clothes and food for the baby. Susan and Jim donated their food rations and, when not at work, Dad foraged for what he couldn't buy. He discovered he could find coal on the railway embankment, fallen from passing trains. The train crews noticed that Dad had become a regular on the embankment and they obliged him by increasing the "accidental" loss of coal from the footplate. Another source of fuel was trees in the park. This was a park in the England my father had fought for and in which no one was helping him, so he would help himself. Jim's brother, Joey, also needed fuel so went out with Dad one night for the tree felling, but he was of a somewhat nervous disposition and took to his heels when the first tree crashed to the ground.

Dad found a slightly better job driving for the Walls Company, delivering meat products to wholesale customers, some of whom occasionally found him "spare" sausages and our family was grateful for this luxury on those occasions.

This was not a good life; the country girl pined for the South and she was losing weight. My father felt this could not be their future and tried to save enough for a train fare south.

I don't think he was a betting man, but he put a small bet on Pearl Diver in the Epsom Derby and it won at 40-1. This must have felt like providence and he took the train. Desperate to find work, he followed any leads and knocked on doors until he found employment running the bars in the Highcliffe Hotel in Swanage. Dad asked about accommodation and was directed to a large house at the top of the hill, owned by a lady who was thinking of letting a couple of rooms. He knocked on her door and, as he

40

explained his situation, jingled in his pocket the coins remaining from his winnings. This reassured her that he could pay the rent and we were able to take up residence with Mrs. Stockley (Auntie Stock) who became a lifelong friend.

Dad was hard working and reliable. He had the good fortune to meet an army major, a Major Mathias, whom he had served under and who, with his sister, owned two hotels in Swanage. My parents were given work running one of the hotels. We lived in Swanage for two summers.

There were plenty of rabbits on the headland just outside the town. Auntie Stock's brother John had a gun and Dad and he would go shooting. The rabbits were a welcome supplement and could be served as chicken in the hotel. It all helped. I don't imagine the guests were fooled by the meat, but, if it tasted good...

Hotel work was satisfactory in the summer but something else was needed for the winter. Dad found work in Christchurch in the Military Engineering Experimental Establishment (MEXE) where Baber Green road laying machines were manufactured. The investment in infrastructure by the post-war Labour government was starting to have an effect on the economy and some work was beginning to become available.

We moved to Christchurch to live in a caravan at Wick on a site known as McArles. The roof leaked, but only when it rained. It was not yet going well. There was little money and only the barest living, but they had each other and they had their determination. And they had me; I was giving them purpose. I was not aware, not a thinking individual. I didn't understand; just lived and took up space and gave them something to work for.

My memories of childhood are very positive. The sun always shone, my mother was always tender and she took me out in a seat on the back of a bicycle. She knitted me clothes and a bathing suit and took me to the beach. She was giving me the childhood she had never had herself. Dad was solid and reliable. He took me fishing and later he bought me a rabbiting dog. When I was old enough to drive, he gave me a motorcycle and sidecar that would enable me to explore my forest and further. He had an expression that he repeated periodically in reflective moments: "If you are going to be poor, be poor in a nice place."

I believe my father was a truly good man, self sufficient, honest, strong willed and reliable. He taught me through example that my integrity was more important than anything else and I have always tried to be absolutely honest in everything I have done. This feels good and helps me to be confident and in control. All I have to do is work for the things I value and then appreciate them when I have them.

We moved again and this time it didn't leak. Dad had found a sort of caravan rented out by a pre-war contact of his, Reg Atkinson. It was actually an old bus that had been converted into a mobile morgue for collecting bodies during the bombing. A stove had been added and it served as a home. This was on the Bure Homage site at Mudeford. I was told much later that I loved to sit in the cab and "drive the bus".

It transpired that this site was not designated for permanent residence and we had to move again.

By this time my mother was, again, at the Kings Arms Hotel, working evenings and Dad was working days.

Rented rooms with a Jane Pixtow were found in Stony Lane, just past Rattenbury's Pool. I later had many happy visits to the pool with my father and stepbrother, Michael. These were fishing trips and we would catch pike, tench and big eels; just the best thing for a young boy.

It was now 1949 and there was an influx of families into the area as men came to work in the expanding de Havilland aircraft factory in Somerford, previously

Airspeeds, where they would build the world's first commercial jet airliner; the Comet. It would go into service with BOAC in 1952.

The National Debt, multiplied by the cost of the war, was more than 200% of GDP in 1945 and increased to 240% by 1947 as additional loans were taken to finance post-war reconstruction. Decades of economic growth were to follow. The predictions of the British economist, John Maynard Keynes, were to proven to be correct and the national debt would fall to 25% of GDP by 1990 in the stimulated economy.

The Labour government's housing programme was building homes up and down the country and a large council estate would be built at Somerford. However, this would take a little time and the council released Nissen huts that had been part of the wartime airfield at Holmsley for accommodation.

The area became known as "Tin Town". Our first hut was in poor condition and constantly had water on the floor. A better hut built of breeze blocks was allocated. This was luxury and Dad equipped it with furniture bought from the Bullstrode's sale rooms in Stour Road, Christchurch.

Our neighbours were a mixture of the incoming de Havilland workers and ex-servicemen with their families.

Dad continued to work at MEXE and Mum now found work at the East Close Hotel which could be reached from Tin Town by bicycle. This job had the great advantage that I could be left with the hotel manager's children in their nursery. Things were looking up: we had the beginnings of a family home and both parents were in work.

Dad met an old associate from his pre-war ice skating days at The Westover Ice Club, A.J. Seal, who told him about a job with accommodation he might be able to secure. This was at the Canford Cliffs Hotel, which was being rebuilt, having been bombed during the war. The accommodation was a flat overlooking the tennis courts and the job was as caretaker and handyman. Some of my earliest memories are from this time. The hotel had extensive grounds and livestock was kept. I can recall accompanying my father as he collected eggs from the chickens and fed the pigs. My mother later told me about a remark I had made – one of those a young child can make when the pages of their worldly knowledge are still blank and waiting to be filled. After collecting eggs, I had asked when the pigs would lay the bacon.

Mum found domestic work in the village, but by Christmas she was working at the Westcliffe Hall Hotel. She was obliged to spend that Christmas working there away from the family. Not ideal, but any honest opportunity to make a little money was taken.

There was an adjacent flat that Dad's younger brother Harry and his wife Ruth took. They too found work locally. Dad then took on additional work as Night Porter at the Norfolk Hotel in Bournemouth.

He must have felt the contrast between this role as a menial in a smart hotel and his life before the war, when he would have been one of the customers being pampered and fawned over by attentive staff who knew their place and hoped to receive a gratuity to supplement their trivial remuneration.

Chapter 5

The Welfare State

By 1950 my parents had moved nine times, gradually working their way up to decent accommodation. They had both worked, often caring for me in shifts. The work was all low paid and temporary, but although everything was bought second hand, they were building a family life.

The building work at Canford Cliffs continued but in the later stages the flats were no longer available and we had to move again. However, the council house building programme was gathering some momentum and homes were being released on the estate at Somerford. Dad rented a flat, number five, Edward Road. This was just opposite the de Havilland factory where he now got a job as a storeman.

I think this was quite a good or, at least, a better period. I remember the de Havilland sports day and fair as a wonderful day out and Dad, of course, won some of the athletic events. Our road was at the very end of the estate and there were fields beyond with the idyllic Watery Lane winding its way alongside a stream and through a boy's utopia. There were blackberries in summer and stickleback and lampreys to be caught. There were lizards in the grassy banks, but I had to be careful not to lift them by the tail. I felt cruel and sad if one shed its tail and I learned empathy with nature. At this time Myxomatosis (myxi) was being used to control the rabbit population and I would occasionally come across a rabbit in the late stages of despair. Why did this happen to these lovely animals?

There was water enough in the stream to float a boat made of balsawood. I made one from a kit and fitted it with a tiny electric motor powered by a 4½ volt battery. I could explore and play all day and discover a magical world.

I knew when I would be expected home for tea; my instruction was, "Come home when you see the Bournemouth Belle." This was the express train on the main line from London to the West Country. A confident steam locomotive pulled its nationalised first, second and third class carriages and the luxury un-nationalised Pullman carriages. Just there, where the line has come through the flood plains of the Avon Valley, its climb over Roeshot Hill is softened by an embankment that carries it high above the fields. It would be clearly visible as it headed to London at 5:05pm with its elongated cumulus of white smoke and steam signalling the end of play.

I wondered who the people were on the train. I'm pretty sure we could not have afforded to travel by train in any class.

London was a place in the North where The King lived. The King was a person in that other world that lived in parallel with mine. We loved The King and my father had fought for him, my grandfather had fought for his father and my great grandfather had fought for his grandmother. I supposed I would fight for him (or, as it turned out, his daughter) when my turn came.

The King and his people were not like us; they were clever and posh, they knew how to run the country and so it was right that they could buy new things and live in big houses. My mother had met some of these special people; they sometimes stayed in the hotels or ate in the restaurants in which she served. She knew how they behaved and she taught me this: how to be polite, how to speak and which knife and fork to eat with; even how to use salt and pepper correctly. This was to be useful later when I grew up and, sometimes, they wouldn't know I was from the second-hand world. With Watery Lane and sticklebacks, I wasn't a lonely child and I didn't realise that most children (it's 80% actually) had a brother or sister, or both. Next door they had three children and they were always fighting, so their situation didn't seem enviable. I enjoyed playing with other children when the opportunity was presented, but I was also happy to amuse myself. I suppose I had learned to be self-reliant. This is a positive consequence of being an only child. The negative is that empathy with others is not learned as naturally without siblings and, in later life, I noticed that I could sometimes offend people with a careless remark or action. This may have been unintentional and it would puzzle me that offence could be taken when none was intended. This weakness in social skills is something I have noticed in other members of this 20%Things got better still; I started school. I was taken to Mudeford School, which is the school my mother had attended. Here there were children to play with and school dinners with gipsy tart for afters. I suppose the population was increasing in Somerford and there was insufficient space for us all at the school. An annex was established in a big house called Sandhills; it was on the beach, which is now called Avon Beach and the beach was my school playground. I was happy at school and seemed to fit in. They made me Milk Monitor. The government wanted children, even from the working class, to be healthy so they arranged for us to have a third of a pint of milk every day and the Milk Monitor would hand this out and show new children how to press the soft cap and take it off. At home I had NHS orange juice and cod liver oil – and a daily spoonful of syrup of figs, just to make sure.

The government had been elected on promises of full employment, a tax funded universal National Health

47

Service and a cradle-to-grave welfare state, with the campaign message "Let us face the future."

Their mission was to tackle want, ignorance, disease, idleness and squalor by acting on the Beveridge Report of 1942, which outlined the requirements for a post-war welfare state. The Keynesian ideas of a managed economy and increased government spending without the need to balance the budget were introduced and the required finance was generated.

In 1950 the Labour government was returned, but with an overall majority of only five seats. The Prime Minister, Clement Atlee, called another election the following year in the hope of securing a bigger majority, but Churchill and the Conservatives were elected, albeit as a minority government with a smaller share of the popular vote than Labour. However, the momentum for change had been established and would continue.

Although the Labour government was relatively short-lived, it had succeeded in changing the social order, initiating a massive programme of social housing, the National Health Service, a reorganised and more egalitarian education system and nationalisation of major industries. I think it is the case that the Conservative Party had elements in it before 1945 that may have supported some of these initiatives, but it is unlikely that change could have been effected by a Conservative government, against the old Tory elements with vested interests. Anyway, people had heard promises during the First World War and little progress had been made, except that the vote had been given to men, and women over 30, in 1918 and to all adults in 1928.

While growing up I had the impression that Britain had always been a liberal democracy, but in fact universal suffrage broad enough to reasonably be called "democracy" was only achieved only 18 years before I was born. We can now see that it produced pendulum politics and, whilst we are making progress, we are still learning how to respond to the aspirations of all our people.

We swing from a centre-left position when we are optimistic or in the mood for social progress and, when times are difficult, we retreat to the old ways that seemed to work before and go back to a centre-right position.

Meanwhile, a boy needed play and other good opportunities were the bomb craters in the area, kindly made for us by the Luftwaffe and now nicely carpeted with soft grass. Here we could play soldiers, or slalom down the sides on homemade soapbox carts or old bicycles. We were warned not to touch anything that could be an unexploded bomb and, occasionally, I would hear of a boy finding one. We were always on the lookout for one of these; it would be a real coup at school.

Two miles out of Somerford, towards Hinton, is the old thatched pub, The Cat and Fiddle, up Roeshot Hill and past Sir George Merrick's Estate. This was Mum's next job and she was to work here for some time. This was just a cycle ride for a fit young woman, but not easy, I think, along that dark road in the winter coming home late at night after the evening shift in the bar. A local artist, H. Lines, did a miniature oil painting of the pub and had it made into a broach as a gift for Mum. She wore it on special occasions and I have it mounted in a frame on my sideboard. I know she regarded it as a special kindness that someone would make such a gift just to bring pleasure to another.

Building of the Somerford Estate continued and we were allocated a house in Druitt Road, at the other end of the estate. Here, Mum made furnishings for the house; she made curtains and a cover and cushions to go over a spare single bed that doubled as settee and guest bed. Dad established a garden where he grew vegetables and kept rabbits for the table.

We had the basics but there were no luxuries. It was rare to see a television, but one family on the estate had one and they would sometimes allow visiting children to watch a programme.

They charged a penny for the privilege and, occasionally, I would join twenty of so children sitting on the living room floor watching Muffin the Mule or some such entertainment.

The picture on the blue one penny stamps I had been saving, one a week, until there were thirty and worth half a crown, changed from George VI's to Elizabeth II's. We celebrated at school and I was given a nice mug decorated with the new queen's picture.

I graduated from Sandhills to the new Somerford Junior School where I made some new friends and we played marbles in the playground. They had a gramophone that played big, brittle records with a needle and trumpet. I had never heard music before and I had no comprehension of what made those sounds. Later, I caught sight of a picture on a small black-and-white television of a man in evening dress waving a baton and he was accompanied by similar music. In my utter stupidity and ignorance I wondered how he could produce all that wonderful sound with a stick.

In evolutionary terms we are much the same animal as our ancestors were 50,000 years ago when they had just began to produce cave paintings to express themselves. How could the same animal be content, or even able, to subsist in a cave, in such a rudimentary manner? Well, I suppose the difference is just education – the passing, down element by element, of what has been learned – and the aspirations it spawns in us. I was just a cave boy, but somewhere in me was the capacity to learn. I might have been slow, but I did eventually acquire a little of the 50,000 years of human knowledge. Later, I got fed up with being called "a late developer". What people meant by this was that they had previously written me off as stupid and were now surprised when they noticed that I was not.

For many years though, until I worked alongside graduates from our best universities, I believed, through my conditioning, that the wealthy were a genetic over-class who had cleverer children.

At Christmas we performed in the school play. It felt good to be with the other thespians, dressing up and having makeup applied. We could see ourselves in the reflection of the classroom windows against the dark sky outside.

I was fortunate to have an inspiring teacher at Somerford Junior; Mr. Wilde. He taught us by rote and I remember most of what he taught me to this day. Tables up to twelve times, mental arithmetic, words ending in *f* have their endings changed to *-ves*, except *chief, dwarf, hoof, roof, reef*, which just gets an *s*. The magic of the duo-decimal system, now denied to modern metric children, was profound in its simplicity and power and I revelled in the speed with which I could calculate the cost of a dozen eggs.

School was becoming more than just play and I was interested in gaining just a little understanding and knowledge of language and arithmetic.

Mr Wilde kept his National Geographical magazines in the classroom store cupboard. These were used to give us, through the beautiful photographic images they contained, an impression of what might lay beyond our horizons. When we boys discovered we could occasionally find a photograph of bare breasted African ladies, the magazines would be surreptitiously scoured for such sinful images – from beyond our horizons.

It was around this time that the Triang trainset I had coveted as I passed the toy shop in Boscombe became the birthday present I had never dared to hope for. It wasn't a Bournemouth Belle express pulled by a Lord Nelson Class 4-6-0 in malachite green with Pullman carriages in umber brown and cream livery, just a black 0-6-0 Class 3F tank engine with four brown goods trucks, but it was too good to believe.

I think I understood even then how many shifts my mother had worked to make that little bit of magic possible for me.

There were redundancies at de Havillands and Dad, with no trade or special aircraft skills, had to find other work. A new secondary school was being built on the field at the bottom of our garden and he worked there as a labourer. At the end of the day he would come home with a wheelbarrow full to the brim with the concrete that was left over after washing out the mixers. Using this, he cast paths all round the garden and it looked good.

Then he worked for Mowlems, on the laying of a pipeline that would take water from the River Avon to the expanding oil refinery at Fawley, 25 miles away.

In 1953, The Somerford Hotel opened at the end of Watery Lane. Mum went to work there as a waitress.

It was around this time that I saw a bit of Michael; he would have been about 18 and he was doing farm work. While he had been at school, Lily had controlled Dad's access to him. The relationship between brother and sister, I think, was tense and, as he had not been in a position financially to provide for Michael as well as Lily had done, I think he deferred to her authority. I remember Dad buying Michael an old motorcycle. I am sure he couldn't afford much, but I do think he was pleased to do a little to show Michael he cared.

The part I remember best is when we three - Michael, Dad and I - went fishing and, as I have mentioned, Rattenbury's Pool was a favourite spot. It was a place that made a boy's heart beat faster. I am not sure whether it was the ambience of the place; there were reed lined banks and dark water with large patches of lily pads seemingly providing cover for marauding giants below.

The three red brick arches that carried the railway line stood against the skyline and painted themselves onto the surface of the water that was sometimes a dark mirror or a shimmering foil, or a moving reflective mosaic.

It may have been the sheer happiness of having Dad in a relaxed mood choosing to spend his time taking me fishing. Or perhaps it was the ghost.

"Don't come here on your own son. There's a ghost."

This was a remote spot; the water was deep and the stems of the water lilies might easily ensnare a careless boy. The ghost should keep me away.

"Mrs Rattenbury. She sat up there." He glanced towards the railings on the parapet of the bridge. "She sat there and stabbed herself through the heart – the heart that was broken when her lover was sentenced to be hanged for the murder of her husband. Her body fell into the water. You can sometimes see her anguished face coming towards the surface in that gap between the lilies or, when the wind gets up, you can hear her crying."

I went fishing alone in the streams, in the Avon River and on the marshes, but never at Rattenbury's Pool. It was fine when Dad was there; you couldn't be afraid of anything.

Fishing on the bottom we caught tench with their full, heavy bellies and orange-brown scales.

"You can't eat these; they are bottom feeders and full of mud."

I could taste the fishy mud as he said it.

We caught pike. The water was deep and there were very big pike in there. On our best days we might catch two or three on live bait, beneath a large cork float. The float would bob and move as the bait struggled, then it would race across the surface as evasive action was taken – and dive deep under the lily pads as a pike struck and ran with its prey to its lair in the depths.

At this point you had to take up the rod from its rest and lift it with a smooth, sustained movement to hook the fish. Too much delay would risk having the rod disappear into the pool; too quick and the bait might be pulled free.We had rods were made out of old tank aerials, purchased from the army surplus shop, but there was one rod that seemed special to Dad and, therefore, to me.

"This is greenheart," Dad would say.

He made it sound like gold or some magic substance blessed by the gods. I think he said this every time he took it out of its old, musky canvas case and tackled it up. It was a ritual that usually guaranteed success.

We could dig in the soft mud of the bank to find large earthworms. With one of the thinner tank aerial rods, a 4 lb. line, a float made from a swan's feather and a number 8 hook, a worm could be used to fish for perch. The pool had big perch that put up an exciting fight. These were handsome fish, up to about two pounds weight and healthy looking, with a spiny dorsal fin and broad, vertical bars of dark brown on yellow scales, fading to silver on the underside.

As a keen fisherman – fisher-boy – I had read about eels crossing fields to get to the next waterway. The marshy approach to Rattenbury's is the only place I can remember seeing this phenomenon. Or, perhaps, I imagined I saw it and filed it in my memory anyway.

"Tell me about Mrs Rattenbury, Dad."

"Ask your mother; she knows the story."

He had said enough. The only use he had for Mrs. Rattenbury's ghost was to keep me safe.

Sometime later I asked Mum about Mrs Rattenbury and she told me the story as she remembered it. When she had been about the same age as I was then – about 8-years-old – her father had arrived home after a day driving his lorry.

He had remarked to her mother that he had seen a strange thing as he drove along Stony Lane. He had seen a lady walking alone along the lane away from the town. He called her a lady because of her smart dress and silk stockings: not the sort of person you would expect to see in that situation. It had struck him as odd.

This was just after one of the 20th century's most sensational murder trials had finished. They were very aware of it in Christchurch; the murder had taken place less than four miles away in Bournemouth.

The Rattenburys, Francis and Alma, had moved to Bournemouth from Victoria on Vancouver Island about five years earlier. Francis was British Columbia's most famous architect and had been responsible for some of their most prestigious public buildings. There was scandal. Alma, nearly thirty years younger than Francis, had been cited as co-respondent in the divorce cases of both her marriage and his. They had chosen Bournemouth as a quiet coastal town with some society, but away from the mainstream, where they could, perhaps, begin again. Francis' health had deteriorated and Alma had an affair with their young chauffer. When Francis was brutally murdered, both Alma and her lover were tried for the crime. Alma was acquitted and the lover sentenced to be hanged.

It was just after her release that my grandfather had seen the woman, whom it transpired was Alma Rattenbury, walking along Stony Lane. They found out the next day that she had climbed to the parapet of the railway bridge over the fishing pool and stabbed herself through the heart before falling into the water.

I don't think the evidence was totally convincing. Both Alma and the chauffer had each initially confessed to the murder to protect the other.

There could have been others involved, but there were no fingerprints on the murder weapon; a wooden mallet. Both pleaded not guilty at the trial. The press pilloried Alma, painting her as an evil older woman who seduced and corrupted a young man. Whatever her part was, it seems that Alma had been full of remorse and took her own life.

Public opinion was so strong that a 300,000 signature petition for leniency for the young chauffer was handed to the Home Office and the sentence was commuted to life imprisonment.

The marine terminal of the refinery was extended to accommodate the new generation of super tankers and, when the pipeline contract finished, Dad worked on the terminal construction. People today complain about Health and Safety but, as a measure of how far we have come, in the 50s and 60s there were normally around a dozen fatalities on a major construction contract such as a power station or a refinery expansion, but now such incidents are rare.

It was on the marine terminal that Dad had his accident. He was knocked off the jetty by a crane as it swung round to make the next pick-up. He fell into the mud. It was low tide, but on the way down he grabbed for the steelwork and a protruding bolt went into his eye. Eyelid and eyeball were split. In Southampton Hospital they sewed him up and sent him home with a bandage. I think this was a very painful injury and he suffered for weeks. The stitches in the eyeball and those in the lid got tangled and I don't think there were drugs available to soften the pain and discomfort. With great good fortune he got through this without losing the sight of that eye, but his wages stopped and there was no compensation.

Mum increased her working hours to support the family and they got through the crisis.

All these years they had been saving up the deposit to buy their own house and the accident was a setback. However, they got through it together. I don't think Dad was able to work for about six months.

One day we were all put on a coach and taken to Twynham School in Christchurch, sat in a big hall and given some question papers. I had not been expecting this and, as far as I recall, I did not answer any questions. I had failed my 11+. Actually, everyone in my class failed, but Geoffrey Hackett, who was the son of our headmaster, was sent to Brockenhurst Grammar School on recommendation. I went to the Somerford County Secondary School that my father built, just at the bottom of the garden.

Michael met a lovely girl, Julia, whom he married. They took the £10 voyage to Australia and started a new life with Michael pursuing his interest in farming. They had a family of seven. There were occasional letters.

Chapter 6

The Alibi

Dad eventually went back to work and, a little later, successfully applied for a job on the Esso payroll as a laboratory assistant. This was fantastic - a permanent job and he would have just enough years to qualify for a pension. He travelled daily on an economical Excelsior 197 cc motorcycle. Saving was the priority and, eventually in 1959, they had their deposit.

A newly built bungalow was found in Thornbury Avenue, Blackfield, just two miles from the refinery. It cost £1800 and it would just be paid for by the time Dad retired. It had taken 13 years, 13 moves and 13 jobs for Dad, 7 for Mum, but now they were buying their home and had a secure future to look forward to. Paths were laid and the garden established. Kitchen cupboards were made using the plywood from used tea chests that could be bought cheaply and it soon became our own home.

Mum found a job collecting insurance premiums for the Prudential Assurance Company. This involved cycling around the villages, 22 miles each day, as Dad registered on his odometer when he drove it just to check. Assurance companies like the Prudential were dependable institutions that people trusted and were happy to pay their premiums, sometimes only a shilling or two a week for basic life assurance or, perhaps, an endowment that would eventually pay for a significant event.

I enrolled at Hardley County Secondary School, which was a cycle ride of two miles and it suited me well. There were capable teachers and an ambitious headmaster.

A small country school would not normally have attracted staff of such calibre, but I think this group saw the opportunity to live in rural idyll as compensation for missing the prestige of working in academically ambitious institutions. Around a dozen of the pupils were identified to be encouraged to take GCE O-Levels; I was one in my year, the second year of this initiative. This just meant that we were streamed, had the more senior teachers and did extra classes instead of games. I got on well with maths and science. I was top of the class in woodwork, but I was taken off that course to concentrate on the more academic subjects. I did manage to learn a bit of history and geography thanks to Mr. Moody who was kind and supportive.

Religious Education was another thing. We didn't have much to do with religion in our family and my father had never been impressed by churchgoers. I think I was a little dyslexic and reading was not a strong skill. One day Mr. Bartlett became so exasperated with me for poor reading of a bible passage that he threw me out of his class. I'm sure he thought I was feigning stupidity, but I do not remember any negative motives on my part, although, I suppose, I may not have been approaching RE with the best attitude.

I got into a few fights at school, but although all the bright kids were at the grammar school, there were only a few lads with a propensity to violence at Hardley. When I did get into a fight it was more a pushing affair and I was never angry enough to want to hurt someone. I had a comfortable home, attentive parents and nothing to be angry about and, even if I was punched, I felt sorry for the aggressor who probably had a less satisfactory home life than I did.

Up to the age of 15 I had been of average height, but then I put on a growth spurt. I had a long stride and found I could run faster than most. Also, my father had been an athlete and I seemed to have inherited some of his stamina. I think it was a surprise to me and also to the PE teachers on the annual sports day when I won most track and jumping events and secured the Victor Ludorum.

Dad bought an AJS 500 cc with a sidecar. The motorcycle combination meant that we could go out as a family and even go on holiday. Dad bought tank suits from the Army and Navy Store, which we used as riding suits.

One day, Dad took me to Totton railway station saying he had a package to collect. The package was waiting for us when we got there. It was a crate with a black greyhound-cross in it. This was to be my dog and Dad had bought him through the Exchange and Mart. He became my close companion and fellow poacher for the next six years. What times we would have together.

The dog was named Certa, which was a corruption of the motto of The Royal Signals. My father was proud of his army service and felt this piece of Latin that he associated with it would be apt. Certa Cito: Swift and Sure.

We went to Cornwall on holiday. That is a long way on the back of an AJS with no rear suspension, but it was worth it; I loved the beaches and seeing another part of the world. The sidecar was a child/adult arrangement. Mum sat in the front and Certa in the back. The poor dog had no hair on his backside by the time we arrived in Cornwall; he had travelled the whole way stood up and rubbing on the seat back.

Mum found a job that was closer to home; this was running the executive dining room at the refinery. Dr. Mayo was the Refinery Manager and in those days they had a smart dining room for the senior managers and business visitors.

There was a dining room for the staff and one for the hourly paid workers that was split into two: one part for those wearing overalls and one for those who without. Everyone knew their place. To enhance its reputation as the best employer in the area, Esso opened a smart social club adjacent to the refinery in Holbury. It had a cinema, dance hall, snooker rooms and restaurant. Mum moved with the executive restaurant to this new location.

A few years later, the position of librarian at the Fawley village library became vacant. Mum applied and, to her surprise, was successful. Presently she was running the library in Blackfield also; three afternoons in Fawley and two days in Blackfield. I think she liked this work; it gave her chance to meet a lot of local people and to do some reading and there was also a little prestige attached to the position of Village Librarian. She became quite knowledgeable about the popular authors and enjoyed helping the customers. At last she was getting an education.

I was also getting an education, but mine was in country ways. We had forest and beaches just a walk or a cycle ride away and there was much to discover.

I loved my forest and the richness of its secrets and learning many of these gave me a sense of belonging; being part of it. I had discovered that the forest stream at Gatebridge, only a walk from the house, was full of trout. These were not big, but two or three grilled on toast made an excellent snack. I used a short child's rod, a simple reel, very light line and a matchstick for a float. The best bait was a small red worm from the compost heap, just floated under the bank in one of the deeper parts of the stream.

I also knew my way around the Drummond and Rothschild's estates where there were rabbits and pheasants to be caught. The landowners had far more than they needed and would not miss what I could take.

I rarely saw a gamekeeper and, when I did, he was easily evaded. Anyway, he could not possibly run as fast as this young athlete and a greyhound-cross.

These were halcyon days, spent mostly solitary, but sometimes with my friend, Tom, with his spaniel-cross; good for finding rabbits for the lurcher to catch. A spaniel hunts with its nose and a hound with its eye; they make a good team. I enjoyed seeing Certa running at full stretch.

I also liked to see the spaniel at work; he would need to keep jumping up to see over the grass to get his bearings and his big ears would appear to flap in attempted flight. When I added a big white hob ferret to the team we could catch as many rabbits as we wanted. The big ferret was much better than Tom's small jill. The smaller ferret was more nimble and would often make a kill underground, then help herself to a meal and sleep it off. This necessitated waiting a couple of hours for the happy animal to re-emerge from the bury.

I sometimes used purse nets; I had about a dozen and would spread one over each hole and anchor the drawstring to the ground with a wooden peg. However, with a greyhound-cross they were not needed if there was open ground around and it was more exciting to see the hound's sinew and muscle alternately folding and stretching in perfect motion as it did its work in pursuit of the quarry.

Rabbits were usually caught within 10 or 20 yards and in open ground they were always caught. A rabbit can only run for about 40 yards at what it hopes is escape velocity. It doesn't have a lot of stamina, having spent its life sat close to cover munching dandelions. A hare is quite different. I have a lot of respect for the hare; it too is an athlete and can run all day. There is a lesson for us all in this; it isn't good to be sedentary.

I don't remember Certa ever catching a hare. He was fast enough but, as well as its stamina, a hare can turn fast, even faster than a greyhound-cross and make the dog overrun if it is getting too close. I actually caught a hare myself on one occasion. I was a pretty good runner, although not in the same class as a greyhound-cross. One evening he put up a hare on the common, in a place where the heather covering was a dense, coarse blanket more than two feet thick. Both hare and dog both had difficulty getting purchase to apply their speed and I was the faster that one time.

Pheasants were a little more difficult but a .22 Airsporter could stop a pheasant silently. No need for a noisy shotgun. The routine was to find a spot near to where pheasants were feeding but behind some cover and secure from a chance meeting with the keeper. Two or three pheasants would be shot and, after checking the coast was clear, I'd run over and pick them up. You couldn't wait too long because a pheasant might be only stunned and may stand up again and run to freedom.

Sometimes I would rest, lying under the sun and just snooze in its warmth in a grassy clearing, listening to the sounds of the brook and the birds and the insects. Even by myself I was never alone in the country. As well as the dog, most seasons would provide a representative of nature to accompany me. The best month was July when, on the walk home at dusk, magic glow worms would signal to potential mates and ghostly nightjars would cruise in the last light of the day, soundless and low, not much above head height. There was often something to entertain me and each season had its special appeal as another creature enjoyed its turn on stage.

This is probably the period of my young life I remember most fondly. Things were going well for our little family. I can only remember affection and support from Mum and Dad.

Our bungalow was always warm and inviting and the garden thriving. There was always something going on in the kitchen; it was a laundry, brewery, factory for producing pickles and jams and the place where the sewing machine ran up curtains, furnishings and clothes.

On washing day the big, sturdy Parnell was pulled into the centre of the floor, charged and activated. Mum would thrust and parry with giant wooden tongs; the machine, with its great oscillating agitator, would counter with menacing shaking and groaning.

Mum would eventually emerge triumphant from the action amidst clouds of steam and the soggy garments and linen would be wrestled into submission and hung out to dry on the clothes' line.

Some days I would come home and sit at the kitchen table with a mug of tea and glance across towards the stove where a pig, with his snout resting on the rim, would be looking out of a large pan, watching me as he was boiled down on his way to becoming pork brawn. Each in its season would be in the making; jam from Dad's loganberries or raspberries, the pickling of his shallots or red cabbage. Quinces would become jelly, apples and plums would become chutney and surplus eggs from the chickens would be put into storage in a bucket of isinglass. Anything that could be created mainly from home produce would be; nothing would be thrown away if it could be mended. We would buy new, only if we couldn't make it or find it second hand. When I needed an apron for the woodwork class, an old bolster was deprived of its cover and I had a splendid, striped apron. Other lads had only plain calico aprons, shop bought and not hand stitched. Mum knew the only way to avoid holes in your shoes, or in your stomach, was to make-do-and-mend and store everything you could. There could be a hard winter or another war at any time and we would be ready.

I had warm jumpers for the winter. There wasn't a local New Forest style so mum scoured the nation for suitable patterns and tried them all. I had Fair Isle and Hebridean, Aran and Cornish fisherman's. There were cardigans, jumpers, waistcoats and jackets with crew necks, turtle necks, polo necks and V-necks, raglan sleeves and square sleeves or no sleeves at all. They were double-knit, single-knit, plain and purl, cable stitch and crochet – all translated from the original to a Molly Morley left-hand variant.

When a hole appeared on an elbow, or other irretrievable wear appeared, the garment would be unpicked and I would have to sit with skeins of wool between my hands and offered so Mum could rewind it into balls for use in the next project. Most lads of my age would have been embarrassed to wear all these knitting exhibition pieces, but I met any implied criticism with a warm swagger. I suspect that some of the creations may have been conceived to test my strength of character or to help me to learn how to fight and, I am sorry to say, I did draw the line at the turquoise and yellow crocheted woollen tie.

I remember getting home from school one day and as I opened the kitchen door the rich smell of one of Mum's casseroles welcomed me in, but there was also tension in the air and the greeting was not what I expected.

"What time do you call this? It's a good job you got home before your father."

I had stopped off with Tom on the way home from school, but that was not unusual and, if Mum had been angry about something, she would have been on the chair behind the door to crack me about the ear with her wooden spoon. This would be the routine for a domestic infringement like: "You left the bathroom in a mess" or "I had to make your bed for you again." The spoon worked well in most situations; it said, "I might be only 5'2" and you're nearly a foot taller, but I am still in charge in this house."

It delivered the message and avoided unnecessary dialogue. I would have been happy with the spoon but felt disturbed by the tension.

"PC Potts called to see you; he'll call back," she said, with concern in her voice.

I knew PC Potts, but we did not have a relationship - yet - and I couldn't think of why I might be asked to "help with enquiries."

Nothing unusual came to mind. I hadn't been cycling on the pavement, or riding without lights and, surely, climbing over the fence at the rec. was not a police matter.

There was the poaching on the Drummond estate on Sunday evening, but I hadn't been seen; I was sure of that. Anyway, I was too careful, too country-wise to be caught.

The forest and the private estates were mine; mine and my dog's and it was the job of a teenage boy to be a poacher. It was expected. Also, Dad wouldn't have bought me a coursing dog if there was anything wrong with it.

While I considered the possibilities, the comfortable aroma of the stew again caught my nose and seeped into my consciousness. I considered this also; rabbit stew was only circumstantial evidence, even if old PC Potts had noticed it.

Just as I was about to ask when the PC would be returning, there was a steady, authoritative knock at the door.

"I'm making enquiries about the theft of strawberries from Drove Farm. Farmer Wiltshire saw the boys himself and he knew who they were. He's sure it was you and that pal of yours."

Relief! I had not been there, at least not at the time of the strawberry crime. True, there had been run-ins with Farmer Wiltshire, but over rabbiting on his land. We never stole produce and we were good poachers, always taking care not to damage fences or leave gates open.

We respected country rules and didn't understand what he had against us.

I was invited to go with PC Potts in his Morris Minor. We called to pick up Tom, then on to Grove Farm.

"Yes, that's them," the farmer stated with confidence, "I know them well."

The interrogation began, "What have you got to say for yourselves?"

"No, it wasn't us."

"Well, where were you on Sunday evening?" demanded Potts, emphasising each word.

The confidence evaporated when I realised the frailty of the alibi.

"We were poaching on the Drummond Estate, but no one saw us," suddenly didn't sound useful or convincing.

We spluttered and floundered – and looked guilty.

There was admonishment, but when Potts was satisfied that his skills as a detective had been demonstrated and the offenders had been intimidated enough, he dismissed them with, "Don't let me catch you again."

Farmer Wiltshire's disappointment that there was to be no custodial sentence was apparent, but he too was ready for his dinner.

I felt the unfairness of being blamed for petty theft and my dad would be disappointed in me. However, he would understand my alibi and I would be able to explain the truth to him as he enjoyed his rabbit stew.

Some days, between Easter and September, I would take an evening off poaching and go to Lepe beach, only two miles away. There was a little bit of sand by the lifeboat station and a raft moored just off shore, for boys to dive from.

Lepe foreshore was mostly stones mixed with dark sandy mud, not the most inviting for beach games, but excellent for digging ragworm for sea fishing bait. Flounders and bass could be caught off the beach. There were cockles and winkles in profusion that could easily be gathered and taken home to be boiled up for a tasty treat. Actually, the winkles were not that tasty and were tedious to eat; each one had to be extracted from its shell with a pin. A lot of work for a tiny morsel, but there was an appeal to gathering them fresh from the sea.

I left school at sixteen with four O-Levels. This was not outstanding and, with the power of education not understood in my family, there was never a suggestion of me continuing at school.

There was no one in my family with experience of tertiary education and everyone I knew had left school at 14 or 15. We never talked about education; just the basics were needed and a boy should aspire to a trade apprenticeship.

I was bright at school, compared with my fellow 11-plus failures at the Secondary Modern. I paid attention in class and enjoyed learning. However, I didn't do homework; there were too many distractions and there was no pressure at home to study.

Now the years of hard work and prudent management of their affairs were beginning to pay off for my parents. They were still saving and were able to go to Hargroves and Babey in Totton and part exchange the minivan for a brand new Morris Traveller; £655 5s 8d. This was 1966. Mum never threw anything away and I found the receipt in her papers after she died. They paid cash of course; I don't think they ever bought anything on credit, except the bungalow.

I think Dad was happy; you could see how much he enjoyed his family, his house, his garden and his car, although he still reminded himself and me, from time to time, "If you're going to be poor, be poor in a nice place." He still needed to be careful with money, but he was no longer as poor as he had been. He did, however, have a regret that he could not address and this, I later learned, disturbed him.

Some years after he died, my mother found a letter in his jacket pocket that he had written to my stepbrother Michael. He had written about his ambition for us to join Michael in Australia but, I suppose, he realised this was not achievable and he never posted it.

He must have always regretted not having been able to give Michael a home, but the war and the circumstances after it had made it preferable for Michael to have the support Lily was willing to provide.

Chapter 7

Get a Trade Son

In the Britain my father had returned to after the war, he had no useful qualifications and had found it difficult to get work, whilst he had seen those with a trade in regular employment.

"Get a trade son," he advised.

He had no experience of education, which he associated with the ruling classes who, in his experience, had not distinguished themselves. There was no thought of me continuing in full time education.

He had brought us to live in an area where an oil refinery was expanding and attracting other businesses and a new power station was planned. This was a good place and time for employment and there were openings for apprentices and trainees.

I was offered apprenticeships with Esso at Fawley, The Central Electricity Generating Board in Marchwood and a Trainee position at the Guardian Royal Exchange Assurance Company in Southampton.

I thought I would like to work outdoors and Dad thought Esso was a good company, so I chose that one. The Generating Board position would have been as "Student Apprentice", which sounded like a higher grade, but Esso offered me day and block release to study both a City and Guilds craft course and National Certificate in Mechanical Engineering. I did the two courses in parallel: craft classes on block release; National Certificate, day release. During the block release periods, I missed one day of the craft classes each week and had to catch up. I passed all my craft exams, achieving the City and Guilds Full Technological Certificate and the Ordinary and Higher National Certificates.

I even had a year spare; the fifth year of my apprenticeship, when I took endorsements in Industrial Law.

This might have seemed to be a heavy academic workload, but I had become quite used to taking exams. At my school the norm had been to take the lower level Royal Society of Arts' exams at age 15 and I did those. Then there were UEI's, a bit easier than GCE's and I took those. Also, because the school was not sure what their "academic" group could achieve, we took Certificates of Proficiency in Arithmetic and English. I passed them all and also achieved four GCE O-Levels, including the important ones in Maths, Science and English. In my spare time I was able to achieve a bronze medal for ballroom dancing, although I only did this so I could dance with girls. I have dozens of certificates.

Further education was worked through satisfactorily enough. As at school, I applied myself in class but rarely spent more time than necessary on homework or extra study. I became a master of the 40% - just what was needed to pass, but not much more, although the craft exams were rather easy and distinctions were achieved in most subjects.

Studies were at Southampton Technical College. Most of my classes were in the new college buildings in East Park Terrace, but initially I went to the old college in St. Mary's Street and it is there I did the first block release. We studied technical subjects and sat at high wooden benches in this Victorian establishment, but they also tried to broaden our minds with Liberal Studies. I met lads from all around the area and this interested me; they were not all country boys like me.

One day, while our minds were being broadened, the lecturer wrote on the board, "You've never had it so good."

Hobbs was a big lad with large feet, a lot of fair hair and a bouncy disposition. He arrived late, as we were struggling to respond to the lecturer's invitation for comment.

Hobbs glanced at the board as he took his seat and solved our problem with his incisive repose, "I've never had it sir," he boomed.

This was just the best reaction to Harold Macmillan's condescending proclamation, resentful as it was of the riches lavished on the working classes by the Welfare State and the social programmes initiated by the post-war Labour government that his party was now trying to reverse. Although he talked about social reform and "one nation" politics, Macmillan appeared to many to be just another pompous old Etonian Conservative, uncomfortable with any sort of working class influence and believing the working man should know his place. After his election victory in 1959, Macmillan had declared, "The class war is obsolete." He might have hoped the class war was over, but he did not give the impression of wishing to see the end of class divisions and privilege and, like all Conservatives, he mourned for the Britain that had been lost; the Britain of privilege and social order that guaranteed everyone their place.

My father had never preached politics to me, but his disdain for the ruling classes had been dripped into me over the years as he commented on the news or observed how some soft handed, white-collared twit had demonstrated his ineptitude in some everyday task. He had seen enough of the upper classes in his skating days to know how shallow and worthless they were and, after the war, how little they cared about those lower down the social structure. There wasn't bitterness, just a stoic get-on-with-it approach to life that left little doubt that this was the way things were. People who said class divisions were disappearing were not from the lower classes.

"No, a working man would be voting against himself if he voted Conservative," Dad had said plainly, when I asked the daft question.

There were no long, inspiring conversations about politics, or about life; there was no obvious indoctrination and, anyway, my father was not a socialist, or in any way political and didn't seem to admire agitators or militant trades' unionists any more than he did the ruling classes. He would demonstrate the virtues of a strong, independent, industrious and honest life – no need to talk about it – and I could follow his example if I chose to.

Dad did insist on high standards of personal presentation. Shoes had to be polished and the attire appropriate to the situation. When I nurtured my adolescent facial hair into a faint beard, this subversive behaviour was met with, "Not in my house, Son" and standards were immediately restored. I never felt afraid of my father, but he had a presence and you didn't argue with him.

Despite his disdain for those with privilege and those of poor character, my father was an optimist with a bright, positive attitude to life; he believed that decency and hard work was in the people of Britain and would prevail. He was patriotic and seemed to have no doubts about the rightness of the war, nor regrets about his army service and he served his employer with the same loyalty.

I enjoyed going to Southampton. In the early years, the journey was a five mile cycle ride to Hythe, to catch the Southampton ferry, which carried foot passengers. There was a small fleet of boats: the Hotspurs I to IV, painted black with cream superstructure. These scruffy, robust little ships were around 30-years-old, but quite suitable for their job. They were boarded by a plank with a rope hand line and had the type of seating on deck that doubled as life rafts. That's where I sat so I could look out for the Queens and other ships as they were escorted by tugs to the docks.

I could also look down the hatch into the engine room where the diesel engine with its polished brass coughed and hissed, sending vibrations through the boat and just enough power to the propellers to carry us across Southampton Water for the 20 minute trip. Most passengers sat in a cabin under the deck where their cigarettes would not burn away so fast out of the wind, but where they would be subject to the noise and the full vibration treatment from the engine.

There was a quaint little 2ft. gauge electric train with three doorless – or the sliding doors were always open – carriages that could take you from the ticket office to the pier-head at Hythe but, actually, I could keep up with it just walking.

From the ferry terminal on the "other side" it was about 15 minutes' walk to the college, past white stone edifices still showing their shrapnel injuries from the 57 Luftwaffe attacks, mostly in the Blitz of 1940 and 1941. It was then through the Bargate, the medieval city entrance and across the park to the college.

The apprenticeship was indentured - a contract between the employer, the Unions and my father. It was for five years and approved by both the Electrical Trades Union (ETU) and the Amalgamated Engineering Union (AEU), because there were sufficient electrical and mechanical elements in it to satisfy both unions. My trade was Instrument Fitter. Other trades were Electrician, Mechanical Fitter, Pipefitter and Boilermaker. For the first year we all learned basic engineering skills in the Apprentice Training Centre. This was very satisfying and I enjoyed the diversity of it. I feel privileged to have had the opportunity to learn so much.

In the refinery there were still pipes and tanks that were of riveted construction, so we learned hot riveting. Smaller pipes were extruded from carbon steel and we learned to bend them by filling with dry sand, for internal support and heating with oxy-acetylene torches before making the bend in a hand powered hydraulic bending machine. We learned how to weld with both gas and electric arc and it was interesting to test work to destruction to see the penetration of a weld; it required a steady hand and good technique to achieve a good weld.

It is satisfying to make useful things from sheet metal by cutting, bending, folding and soldering and we did this. Tool boxes, coal scuttles, funnels and other useful items were produced.

We did electrical wiring and electronics - this was before transistors had come into general use - and all circuits used thermionic valves; those clever little glass tubes in which the electrons from a heated cathode can be made to flow free to the anode in a controlled manner to achieve amplification or modification of signals.

There was a well equipped machine shop with lathes, milling machines, grinders and power saws where the preparation of work pieces and tools and machining of different metals was practised. The lathe is a versatile machine tool that can produce complex metal parts with threads, chamfers or knurled finishes.

The bench fitting shop might have seemed the most mundane - just using hand tools - but this, perhaps, is where the greatest engineering trade skill was found. The first exercise was to start with a piece of rusted mild steel plate and, with only vice, file, micrometer, rule and tri-square make it into a simple square prism. It had to be two inches square and one quarter of an inch thick with all corners right angles - and all within one thousandth of an inch.

After hours of diligent work, the masterpiece would be offered to the venerable instructor who would, of course, reject it. It would be thrown contemptuously against the stone floor where the impact would bruise a corner such that it could not possibly be re-worked to meet the specification. We would start again with another piece of rusty steel. The best among us achieved specification in about three attempts; the less adept needed seven or eight tries. I can still file straight.

The metal benches were fitted with an engineering vice, one each side and towards one end, such that two of us stood diagonally across the bench from each other. I shared my bench with Roger, who had come from the grammar school. We didn't have many grammar school boys, but Roger was a free spirit and had found social life, rugby and alcohol preferable to the pursuit of academic excellence; he was bright but undisciplined.

My end of the bench was kept clean and my files arranged in a neat fan so I could, like a brain surgeon, select the right tool for the current operation. Roger's end was chaos: a jumble of tools, iron filings and discarded, torn emery paper. It annoyed Roger to see my organisation and, after a couple of days, he lent across and scrambled my tools into an untidy heap. I stopped work and re-ordered them. He disordered them. The cycle was repeated a few times. This was Roger's idea of a diversion from the tedium of this repetitive exercise and I was more amused than angry about his intrusions. I advised, however, that, if he did it again, I would thump him. Not doing it again was not an option for Roger. Schopenhauer was right: there is no free will. To play my part and to continue the joke after a further transgression, I struck him on the chin with my fist. There was no serious damage done, but I had hit him harder than I intended. He agreed not to do it again and I agreed not to be so tidy.

Sometimes, when people are thrown together in adversity and, only by their strength of character, successfully face a common enemy, a deep and lasting bond is formed. So it was with Roger and me and, over the next years, we would regularly share the ritual that young men share during their passage to manhood: pointless drunkenness.

We had three full-time instructors who probably, for their own sanity, occasionally retreated to the canteen for a break. When left alone, the mature young adults, gratefully learning a trade, would transform into mischievous, irresponsible hooligans, as if possessed by evil spirits under a full moon. One apprentice was squeezed into a slim metal locker, which then had its door welded closed, using the newly acquired skill with a gas torch. Another was strapped to the table of a milling machine, which was then put onto automatic feed with a large side cutter running and only stopped when the torturers lost nerve and relented.

During the following four years I worked on many of the refinery and chemicals plants, the tank farms and the marine terminal. The refinery had been built in 1935 by the AGWI Company and some of the old processing units were still in existence. My career in industrial automation was to span from the very first remote monitoring and control systems, through several generations of mechanical, hydraulic, pneumatic and electronic instruments to computer control. I was an enthusiast and, by the time I had finished my apprenticeship, I had gained an encyclopaedic knowledge of the equipment in the way that some boys accumulate knowledge of trains, aircraft or cars. The technical aspect of the work was absorbing and enjoyable, just like playing with a giant Meccano set.

Dad bought a car. Actually, it was a second-hand minivan. Vans were cheaper because the purchase tax was lower than that for a car. This one had been purchased in primer paint only, to further reduce the cost and been hand painted by the original owner.

The AJS was no longer needed for family transport and it became mine. I was sixteen and learning to drive on a motorcycle combination; a significant step in my personal development. It was a very odd thing to control at first and it needed a lot of confidence to go round left hand bends, which created the feeling that the sidecar would rise into the air uncontrollably.

It was ideal for my needs, however, and I could extend my poaching range to all parts of the New Forest. Certa was quite used to this transport and seemed to positively enjoy our rides together. I discovered a large bury on the heath between Lymington and Beaulieu, set the purse nets and introduced the ferret. After a short interval, the sound of underground activity could be heard like a dull thunder. Rabbits rapidly filled the nets, displacing them so that their following brethren ran free, some of which were intercepted by the dog. This was an orgy of rabbit catching and I did not notice the approaching keeper who pulled up my nets and confiscated them before departing abruptly. The loss of the nets was unwelcome but I had to bear it.

When I returned to the same spot a couple of weeks later, it seemed perverse that the bury had been gassed in a controlled cull of the rabbits. It didn't seem sensible or efficient to deny a country boy his harmless sport and then deploy ugly tactics to control the rabbit population. I resented that those with privilege acted this way just to keep me in my working class place. Such experiences put a chip on my shoulder, a suspicion of authority that would later hold me back until I would eventually prove to myself and others that I could hold my own in any company.

Chapter 8

The Motorcyclist

Around 1965, Dad came home from a trip to Southampton brimming with excitement. "Come on, I've found you a smashing bike. It's with a car dealer: a Matchless twin they took in part exchange for a car and just want to pass it on; only £80 and hardly any mileage."

I couldn't have argued with him if I had wanted to. It was an excellent buy and the most I could afford with the savings from my wages – £5 2s 6d a week: £2 housekeeping for Mum and the rest for transport, clothes and leisure. We took the bike home and fitted the sidecar; necessary to transport the dog and much safer, as Dad advised.

At times I would take the sidecar body off and bolt a plywood platform to the chassis. My friend, Alan, would ride on the platform and we would race round the forest roads pretending we were on the Isle of Man at the TT Races.

One evening, as I was relaxing at home, Alan knocked at the door, then burst in.

"'Ose is dead," he said. This was a difficult message to absorb.

'Ose, Nigel Hosey, was a motorcycling friend, the same age as me. He had joined the army to extend his horizons and, after a spell posted somewhere in the East, he had been taken ill with what they told him was a tropical illness and sent home. In fact he had leukaemia for which the prognosis was very poor at that time. I think we all knew this and it had been difficult visiting him in hospital. It was still a shock when he died; the first experience of death for most of our group.

I thought a lot about 'Ose and about myself too. I hoped I would achieve more before my end came. I hoped I would have children. Is this a basic survival instinct?

A couple of us went camping in Swanage. I went to the chemist to buy some Durex so I could start practising now there was some urgency. This was a time in which masturbation made you go blind, sex was unhealthy and people pretended it didn't happen outside marriage. The buying of the Durex was, therefore, not straightforward for a teenage boy. I suppose this routine was repeated in chemist shops up and down the land. You cased the joint to determine that the assistant was not a young girl or, worse, a matronly woman; you came back at a time judged to be a quiet period so there should be no one behind you in the queue; you approached confidently with a contingency plan and if conditions were not right you would ask for a packet of Tunes or some Aspirin. Eventually, with Tunes and aspirin in your pocket, you would return and ask for the taboo items; "gossamer" would be asked for specifically to avoid the need to stammer out a reply if asked to choose "gossamer" or "featherlite" and the right money would be handed over to avoid unnecessary delay. They came in packets of three and I carried that packet in my wallet for ages, perhaps hoping to use one, perhaps just as a reminder of a passage to manhood that would one day be achieved.

The only other place to buy Durex was the barber's shop where the older men would routinely be asked, "A little something for the weekend, sir?"

For a teenager, however, the risk of being the butt of the manly humour that would surely follow would have been unthinkable. It would be a couple more years before pub toilets would evolve to provide anonymous machine dispensing capability.

I started to use my motorbike for the journey to Southampton Technical College. This saved some time and it was a pleasant ride except on the coldest days of the winter. There was generally a traffic hold up after about eight miles, on the Totton flyover. This was a welcome opportunity to stop and put my hands on the cylinder head to warm up. Even with this mid-journey heat input, my hands would be so numb when I reached the college that I couldn't write 'til around 10am when they had thawed sufficiently to get the feeling back.

When we had first moved to Blackfield, the journey to Totton, at the head of Southampton Water, took an hour by bus. After the Marchwood by-pass was built and I had acquired the Matchless, I could do it in eight minutes, although I shudder to think of that now and I feel fortunate to have survived that motorcycling period.

It was probably an evolutionary advantage for our species that its young men were endowed with incautious confidence and an inability to see danger. It was this that informed my approach to motorcycling. Although I rode at high speed, I was always in perfect control, alert and resourceful. I planned for any eventuality and I would go a bit faster if sliding off on a bend would just take me into a field or through a relatively benign looking hedge. If I did unexpectedly meet a car coming the other way I could stand up on the footrests and fly gracefully over the other vehicle without sustaining injury. This theory was born out the day I was riding pillion on Tom's bike and the Morgan sports car we were overtaking in Holbury suddenly turned right. There was no time for evasive action but, on impact, I flew over the handle bars, over Tom, over the Morgan and gracefully slid down the road, which had helpfully been lubricated by a good rain fall. The shell of my Corker helmet was cracked open and my spitfire pilot's goggles and the peak of the helmet, which had folded down to protect my nose, were nearly ground away.

My only injuries were scratches on each shin where I had just caught the bike's control levers during my airborne phase. I did have a few more crashes but never sustained serious injury and the scars have faded.

As it happened, the Morgan crash occurred the weekend before I moved to a new plant in the refinery - the cat cracker. I reported to the control room on the Monday morning to introduce myself to my new boss and when I met him, he was...the Morgan driver. This was a slightly awkward moment and I was grateful that I had been too shaken after the crash to be impolite. Our relationship received further strain when the local newspaper later reported that he had received a fine and driving licence endorsement for his part in the accident. However, neither of us seemed to have any animosity over the incident and I think his behaviour slightly softened my antipathy towards the ruling classes. Here was a young man with a public school education and a good degree from Imperial College – behaving sensibly.

The Morgan driver was a control engineer whose role it was to commission the new refinery computer control system. Actually, this was the world's first multi-plant computer control system. Morgan driver introduced me to the Zeigler-Nicholls equations, which could model the behaviour of real processes and enable the engineer to optimise the control algorithms. I had learned from the Fitters how to do this empirically, but here was someone who knew how to do it mathematically. In practice, the mathematics didn't work as well as my trial-and-error method. When I later had enough mathematics myself I realised why. The real world has a quirky little feature built in – hysteresis – that thumbs it nose at mathematics. Actually, the best results are achieved by using the maths with a bit of trial-and-error. Morgan driver and I were a good team.

Motorcycling can be liberating for a young man. It opens a door to the world and allows easy travel, but there is more. There is a great sense of freedom and life, the universe and everything can be contemplated from the saddle.

I have had just a few experiences in my life that I have not understood. One of them happened on a bike. A more emotional person might ascribe deep significance to this, but I am happy to just say that I can't explain it. I'll describe the situation as I remember it.

I opened the shed door and it stood there, waiting. I lifted my left leg over the saddle and stood astride the machine, then rocked it forward; just a little pressure gets it off its centre-stand and it settles onto both wheels. I sit, still with feet on the ground and push backwards out of the shed. Half a turn and I'm facing in the right direction.

Flick on the petrol tap, wait a few seconds, prime the carburettor, rotate the choke lever and it's ready to have life breathed into it. Right foot on the kick-start, a little pressure to find top-dead-centre and the fingers of the right hand just holding the front brake on. A single downward swing of the foot and it should start. It should start because it is cared for; a machine in prime condition. If it didn't start there would be disappointment.

It's a smart machine, well maintained, clean and shining, but not over polished, not a display thing; a machine to be ridden by someone who understands it.

To understand the machine, a thing outside yourself, is a step to understanding more of the universe, more of creation.

It does start. After half a minute the choke is opened, taking the hesitation out of the exhaust note; the clutch is pulled in and first gear engaged with an upward flick of the right toe. Let out the clutch gently and we're off, through the gate, down the road and into the world.

On a good motorcycle, you have the whole world at your feet – at your wheels.

Out of the village, onto the open road and, after ten minutes, the engine is warm and coming on song. On a morning like this, with the mist still lying in the lower levels, the engine is happy; those tiny droplets of water add efficiency to the transfer of chemical energy to mechanical, as the petrol, air (and mist) mix in the Amal monobloc carburettor and undergo rapid combustion after compression in the cylinders.

There is no God. There is no room for God in modern society. Science has all the answers.

Approaching the next village and here is a service road for the parades of shops, interspersed with houses. There are occasional breaks in the reservation between the two roads to let the local traffic join the through road.

A slight left-hand bend, I draw gently on the right handlebar. If you haven't ridden a serious motorcycle it may seem odd that you pull the right bar back to turn to the left; it's all to do with the tyre profile, fork angle and lean of the machine. The centripetal acceleration as I take the bend snugs me closer into the saddle and the suspension compresses, just a bit. It feels good; it feels skilful. Perhaps I'm going a bit faster than this road deserves, but I'm alert and on song, like the engine.

Atheists think Christians think that God is an old man with a long, white beard, resting on a cloud. Only Michelangelo thought that.

There's a saloon car just in front. Squeeze the throttle to give a bit more speed and pass it smoothly. There's another car coming towards us but there's room and the extra speed should get me past before the cars draw together.

Everyone believes in God; it's just that some see Him differently and don't recognise Him. Like the blind men feeling an elephant and each describing a different part.

Shit! There's another car coming off the service road. The driver's not looking. Won't make it! He'll join the main road at the same time as the passing cars, at the same time as I squeeze between them. The bike wasn't going to get past the first car before the other arrived, but I could have squeezed through; that is, I could have squeezed through if that silly old fool from the service road wasn't going to hit all of us.

What science has done is to teach us that God is not supernatural. There is a perfectly rational explanation in physics and it won't be too long now before we work it out.

I always had an escape plan because I was a resourceful motorcyclist and, at 19-years-old, I was indestructible. In this situation, I would stand up on the footrests just at the point of impact and I should fly over the cars. My beautiful bike wouldn't though. It's amazing how much time there is for analysis when disaster is imminent.

This is it. Ready...

What happened?

The cars are all behind me; the road ahead is clear. I don't see any clouds. The engine sounds right, the bike feels right.

Explain that.

One winter, I was assigned to the Tankgauging Team. There were three of us: two qualified fitters and me, the apprentice. I was given a Vespa motor scooter to cover the distances around the tank farms. Our job was to keep the tank level gauges working. The most common level gauge was the Varek, which had an electronic sensor that hovered just above the contents of a tank and transmitted information to the control room. The weight of the sensor was carried by a steel tape connected to a drum in a casing outside the tank at ground level and balanced by a "negator spring". This was as long as two tank heights (around one hundred and fifty feet), but was tightly coiled like a steel tape.

87

It had a habit of slipping off its drum and had to be rewound by hand. This operation could take nearly an hour and, in sub zero temperatures, was quite an ordeal as gloves didn't allow sufficient control and couldn't be worn. On the coldest days, it seemed, the negator spring would slip off when fully coiled - just as it was being finally pushed onto the drum - and it would wind itself around your arm like a boa constrictor. I would then unenthusiastically have to start the whole operation again.

Safety was in the dark ages compared with practice by the time of my retirement. I handled mercury, asbestos and many carcinogenic chemicals. I had a permanent ringing in my ears from the noise and continuous catarrh from the pollution. When I worked on the lube oil additives plants, the offensive smell of Paranox was so pervasive that it could not be washed from my hair and skin. As the apprentice, it was me who they dressed in the rubber suit and lowered into the tank to retrieve a disconnected level gauge float, so I got pretty close to the stuff. This had a negative, but thankfully temporary, affect on my social life. At that time I noticed the girls I would sit next to attempting to make friends with in the social club would carefully move away. I was happy about moving on from that assignment.

The most common of the refinery instruments was the mercury manometer, which had a heavy cast iron body in which a float sensed the displacement of mercury in response to differential pressure. Overhaul was required periodically when corrosion and contamination started to inhibit operation. We later learned of the toxic, brain eating effects of mercury and I realised why Old Len, who had worked for more than twenty years in the mercury bay where the overhauls were done, was simple minded.

There were serious injuries and fatalities from time to time and one of my fellow apprentices died relatively young of asbestosis. He had been a pipefitter, a trade that dealt more than the others with asbestos, which insulated the miles of refinery pipes.

I don't think people, generally, appreciated the hazards of work in such places but, as Macmillan had told us, we had "never had it so good".

There was an upside, however, in that the sulphur and ammonia plants were good to visit if you had a hangover; your head would soon be cleared by those toxic but refreshing vapours.

Britain had been "The Workshop of the World" in the 19th century and had continued to be a leading industrial nation, but it failed to modernise the work practices that had been effective, probably until the 1930s. In the post-war world, the United States of America, Germany, Japan and other countries were investing to establish a new industrial base. British industry was hampered by ineffective leaders who had obtained their positions through unearned privilege, complacency, restrictive work practices and lack of investment. By the time I started work in 1963, the defects were beginning to show. Lack of vision and class antagonisms held industry in a time-warp and one industry after another crumbled until successful British owned and managed manufacturing companies became rarities.

At Fawley refinery, which was a "closed shop", enlightened (American) management created a rare oasis in the desert of indifference that was British industry. There had been restrictive practices and over-manning, but an agreement that became famous in industrial relations, The Fawley Blue Book, was accepted by the unions and the way to modernisation was opened.

Disputes were generally resolved without industrial action and the company had an effective method of dealing with troublesome shop-stewards: they promoted them into staff positions and these "poachers" became "gamekeepers".

Also, absenteeism was not a serious problem. There was a company medical centre with doctors and a team of male nurses. You were allowed to take up to three days' sick leave without a doctor's note, but you would be interviewed by one of these male nurses. Such an interview was overheard in the queue one morning as an overalled miscreant claimed his "easy three", as it was known.

"You've been out three days; what has been your problem?" asked the inquisitor.

"Sickness and diarrhoea, *Nurse*."

"And when did you first notice you had this?" asked the nurse wearily.

"When I got home and took my trouser clips off," was the laddish reply.

An employee could take the "easy three" once or twice a year, but if the nurses were not satisfied of the validity of the ailment, a referral to a doctor would add scrutiny. Those who wished to do so could get away with occasional days off like this, but habitual absenteeism was discouraged.

One lunch hour I had been out on the Matchless and rounded the turn at the refinery entrance too fast. Well, too fast, because there was loose grit on the road. I slid off and my left knee took the impact of the fall, then scraped along the road giving me a large gash that filled with grit. With some misgivings I went to the medical centre that was handily located just across the road. I got the nurse with pebble spectacles and a sadistic disposition.

"I can clean that up for you, laddie," he chuckled, barely under his breath.

He took a scrubbing brush and, yes, he got all the grit out. It did make my eyes water, but I was not going to give him the satisfaction of crying out. I still have a big blue scar on that knee.

My next experience of death was when I lost Certa. There were a few lime pits in The Forest and he somehow ran into one chasing a rabbit. The lime burned his hair off and badly affected him such that he contracted pneumonia and just lay in his box until he faded away. I had lost a close friend and it hurt.

I think this coincided with an increasing curiosity to explore further afield and the motorbike put the whole country at my disposal. I went camping in Dorset, Devon and Cornwall with friends and I visited family in Hampshire and Lancashire. We attended motorcycle races at Thruxton and Brands Hatch.

We visited all the pubs in the New Forest. A motorcycle was ideal for this and it had not been considered, at least not by me, that alcohol could in some way impair my judgement. Actually, like most people, I was a better driver after a couple of pints. This was before the campaign of education for drivers and the introduction of a legal blood alcohol limit in 1967.

In 1966, my cousin, John and I agreed to "do the Dragon Rally".

A cold coming we had of it, just the worst time of year. The Dragon Rally wasn't T.S. Eliot's journey of the magi, but it was a journey. Bob, Paul and I set off from the south coast on Triumph, BSA and Matchless. John, my cousin and his pal, Peter, rode from their Manchester suburb on Norton and Triumph and we met on that draughty Welsh hillside.

This was one of only around a dozen meetings with John in a lifetime, but we get on well, pick up where we left off and talk about life. Well, we talk about life now, but then we talked about motorbikes.

How does this happen? Blood is thicker than water? We just happen to share similar aspirations and ideas, the same comfortable baby-boomer existence and underlying restlessness to understand. Understand what? Life I suppose. Bob's and Paul's searches later took them to Australia as young men. I wonder how life has been for them.

Extreme ironing hadn't been invented then so we settled for extreme biking. We thought it made people tut or swoon and we looked menacing in our greasy motorcycling clothing and Autocycle Union approved Everoak pudding-basin racing helmets – just like John Surtees wore.

The second weekend in February and it rained and rained and rained. After five or more hours in those conditions the Belstaff waxed cotton riding suit becomes completely porous. After a few hours you get used to the discomfort and cold and just put up with it.

I earned a licence endorsement on that trip in 1966, just a week after they introduced the 70 miles per hour limit. I like to think I may have been the first. What an achievement that would have been. Or is there more to life? Hadn't I suffered enough and what did Barbara Castle know? She didn't even have a driving licence and I was indestructible. I don't think the Austin Westminster of the Gwynedd Police would have caught me if I hadn't stopped to wait for Paul and Bob. I think they took advantage; it wasn't really a fair cop.

My tent was ex-WD made from 8oz duck canvas, no ground sheet and lots of draft. That was a cold night, with the bottom of my bargain priced sleeping bag torn open and my feet, which were more than six feet away, sticking out. John's tent was all together more middle class: Blacks best lightweight pyramid tent with sewn-in ground sheet. It didn't strain our friendship.

In those days I didn't think in terms of T.S. Eliot or anything towards the literary or cultural, but I seem to have become more inclined to search for words and devices to assist thought and reflection and, after a further 40 odd years of life, work, travel, reading and meeting people from outside my village, there is an appreciation for life's richness and surprises that a teenage motorcyclist from a small rural community could only have guessed at.

Chapter 9

Smokin' an' Drinkin' an' Rowin'

And so I studied a bit, poached a bit, became a motorcyclist. I started to have a social life – Saturday nights at the Esso Social Club.

I learned to drink: Watney's mild, 1s 7d a pint. I learned to smoke. This was because everyone at work smoked and you were allowed to take a smoke break twice a day and go to a "safe" area in the refinery. Smoking was not bad for your health in those days; in fact it killed germs. I quite liked smoking, but the most satisfying part was rolling the cigarettes using Sun Valley tobacco. Sometimes I would use liquorice papers to add some flavour and make me look like Clint Eastwood in The Good, The Bad and The Ugly. If you smoked tailor made cigarettes, you had to have plain, not tipped, because tipped cigarettes were effeminate and the only thing more suspect was menthol cigarettes. These were for "girls" (effeminate boys); girls didn't smoke.

A little later on I took up competitive rowing and I did feel that, perhaps, the smoking affected my performance. Anyway, I wanted to win, so I gave up the smoking just in case it was a factor. I had discovered a competitive streak that would drive me to many successes in sport and career later on.

I joined Lymington Rowing Club, located in a tin shed a hundred yards from the Town Quay where the coastal fours could be launched. A favourite training run was down the river and across the bay to Hurst Castle. On the return, we would look for the Isle of Wight ferry and time our approach to the river so we could race the ferry home; it berthed just across the river from the quay.

In those days, the ferry was a paddle boat that would set up a rolling wave astern. If we got onto this we could surf along with little effort and then, with a hundred or so yards to go, we would engage our saved energy, pull out and race past. Alongside the ferry, an enormous paddle wheel thrashed and crashed through the water and seemed to draw us towards it; it felt dramatic. We would always get past and receive a congratulatory toot on the horn from the skipper.

One evening we set off into the sun as it descended in a clear sky towards Hurst Spit, doing its last work of the day. We were enjoying a fine row when the sky darkened, the wind got up and, as the sea grew ragged, water started to crash over the boat. There was nothing to worry about; those boats have a sealed buoyancy tank fore and aft that can sustain the crew. However, we seemed to be getting lower in the water. We did not think much about safety or care of the equipment and we hadn't been concerned about a tear in the canvas covering the bow tank. It became hard to maintain direction against the strengthening wind and our mood changed for the worse when one oarsman confided that he couldn't swim. The coxswain now owned up that neither could he.

Five lads, a thunderstorm and a couple of miles to row against a hostile wind in a sinking boat.

Presently the two boys at the bow end no longer had sufficient freeboard to be able to row and the stroke, at the stern, just made us go in the wrong direction with his oar being on the windward side. So it was down to me, the three-man, to apply motive power and we slowly progressed towards the mudflats. When the boat eventually succumbed and sank below the waves we found we were on the bottom and could just stand. We scrambled ashore where the estuary mud was so soft and deep it was impossible to walk; we could only crawl and drag the old boat with us, probably still a mile or so from dry land.

We didn't race the ferry that evening.

There is a cosy little pub not far from the rowing club and they didn't mind a bit of singing and revelry on

Saturday evening when we had returned from a regatta. Lymington had 35 pubs, but the Chequers was the most accommodating. It was also quite near the sailing club whose members were middle class; coastal rowers were working class.

One evening, a couple of attractive girls in sailing jackets strayed into the pub. It transpired that one of them, at least, wanted to meet a boy and we got chatting. She proved to be very friendly and I was invited back to the flat she had borrowed for the weekend. This had been fairly late in the evening and we were in a relaxed mood. We discussed water sports and had a pleasant time.

The Swinging Sixties was not a working class phenomenon, at least not in rural areas. With my peers I was too busy moving into work and part-time education to smoke pot, drop out, protest, or experiment with free love. This was apparently done by middle class folk, perhaps with a few urban working class kids who had won the 11+ lottery to go to grammar school and brush with the more privileged. Well, I brushed with the more privileged that evening – and swung a bit.

This was the first time I had been in such a comfortable situation with a girl with her own flat and, although I was surprised by her friendliness, it was a good experience. She too seemed happy with the arrangement and then wanted to take me to the sailing club, where I learned she had argued with her boyfriend and wanted another man to help get her own back on him. I think she may have hoped for me to have a more physical exchange with the boyfriend, but he, like me, was quite mellow at the late hour and the evening passed without further incident. I had thought I had been cool with a winning chat-up line; I did not realise I was just her bit of rough for the evening.

Perhaps I was exploited by one more confident and more used to taking what she wanted but it provided a little education on a Saturday night in a country town.

I had begun to question the social order as I started to notice unearned privilege and that those enjoying it seemed to be receiving more for doing less. I also wondered about those who experienced a measure of negative discrimination in our society. I suppose attitudes in that place were parochial and I had not experienced much diversity. We were all white and comfortably working class with just one black family in our area.

It was generally thought that blacks were not the same as us and there was no understanding of human genetics to discourage those who claimed we were separate species. Similarly, it was understood that men made decisions and earned the wage. Women worked, if they could, to supplement the family income, but should not expect to be treated as equals. Homosexuality was unnatural and unpleasant and was illegal until 1967.

I think I felt intuitively that there was probably no reasonable basis for racial discrimination. I have welcomed the more enlightened thinking that has developed throughout my lifetime. This is encouraging evidence that we are progressing on our journey of social evolution.

It was obvious that girls were more mature than boys of the same age and they were as good at the subjects I studied at school; there is not apparently an intellectual difference attributable to gender. I couldn't imagine ever working for a woman but, otherwise, I could see no good reason for them to hold an inferior position to men in society. Again it feels healthy that attitudes have progressed so much.

I have probably never shaken off that learned suspicion of homosexuals and I still feel the practice should be discrete and not celebrated; it is difficult to erase our social conditioning. I am pleased to see that my children, grown up in a different age, are not coloured by such prejudices.

It takes time and experience for social attitudes to change and we are making progress. I think we have learned that our differences are strengths and accepting the diversity in our society gives us the opportunity to engage all the talents available. Also, we are developing a certain maturity in our attitude that allows our acceptance of others, different to ourselves, to be less effort and less seen as tolerance.

The Matchless increasingly took me to the Concorde Club. This was in the backroom of the Basset Hotel in Southampton where rhythm and blues bands played. Jimmy James and the Vagabonds, Long John Baldry, Eric Clapton; the sixties did begin to swing a little. This was a superior type of music, not like the pop music that girls screamed about; more for serious drinkers and discerning students of life.

I spent a wonderful week at Southampton University during the last year of my apprenticeship. This was another attempt at mind broadening, this time as part of Esso's apprentice training programme. With my peers we attended a residential course during the university holiday period. A few post graduate students were persuaded to join with us for a week of liberal studies. The classroom sessions were interesting enough, but the best were the discussions late into the night during which we tackled the world's problems. This thinking, debating and exchanging ideas was far removed from anything I had experienced before in education and it did hint at new possibilities for me. I started to read literature with a social message: Huxley's Brave New World, Orwell's Down and Out in Paris and London and others of his, Tressell's Ragged Trouser Philanthropists, The Rise of Red China, Marx on Economics and books about Lenin.

Unfortunately, this seemed to sharpen my resentment of the ruling classes rather than helping me to be open minded and it would be some time yet before I would begin to achieve something approaching a balanced view of life.

Back at the refinery, my academic achievements earned me a position in the engineering office, working for the refinery's resident Instrument Engineer, Rex Clark, on the design of plant improvements. Rex was encouraging and helpful and I learned a lot under him.

My apprenticeship drew to an end and I now felt happier in the design office than on the refinery plants and the idea of designing new systems had more appeal than maintenance work. I briefly entertained ideas of continuing to work with Rex, but Esso had a rigid policy that insisted on an engineering degree for staff positions in the design office. They were able to attract graduates from the best universities and would not give a place to an apprentice, even one with a good record and proven ability to do the work.

I felt there was no option but to look elsewhere, but I also had a growing curiosity about the rest of the world. I had spent my childhood and formative years in a country area that was comfortable and secure. In a way I envied my friends in The Forest who were content to be living in a good place and did not feel the need to explore, but I wanted to see what else there was. Moving away was not a carefully considered choice, more a feeling and an impulse. Schopenhauer was right again?

I spotted a job with the Gas Board, an engineering assistant on a new naphtha reforming plant in Croydon. I applied successfully and went to "The North". Everywhere was "north" from a corner of England as far south as you could get without getting your feet wet and connected to the world only by lanes and minor roads. I launched myself on the world but my parents, steady and supportive, would still be a lifeline and I could bring my washing home; it was not so far away on a Matchless twin.

Chapter 10

On a Man's Wage

The naphtha plant had been commissioned, but there was still much to sort out and the maintenance team were relatively inexperienced, giving me opportunity to apply the skills I had learned during my apprenticeship.

Shortly after I arrived, the Queen visited for the official opening of this landmark installation in Britain's energy policy of the day. The new plant was on an old site, adjacent to a Victorian coal gas plant, originally built in 1867. Even though this was scheduled to be demolished, all the parts Her Majesty would pass were spruced up and painted. This was a lot of work and must have been costly. What a waste! I still don't think I understand why we do this. Wouldn't Her Majesty like to see her country as it really is?

One of the brightest and most knowledgeable of the maintenance fitters was handicapped with a very severe stammer. You had to be patient to find out what he had to say and, sometimes, may not be rewarded. One of the plant operators suffered with Tourette's Syndrome and could populate the stammerer's spaces with his own special superlatives when they were in "conversation". The potential for one of life's richest moments was lost when it was somehow decided that this pair would not be presented to the Queen. Just think about it; build that missed moment for yourself... and enjoy it.

My pay was modest, but I needed somewhere to live and I found digs with a Metropolitan Police Sergeant and his family in south Croydon. This served my needs well enough and they were good people. The sergeant was on the Kray twins' task force and I enjoyed getting his updates on progress, usually prefixed by "We're going to get them," the policeman's voice tensed with enthusiasm.

Up to that time, it had seemed that the Krays were untouchable and, even with my distrust of authority, I could see that a society in which these violent yobs could control a part of a major city was not what we would prefer. They did get them, but I think it took a lot of concentration and a raising of their game by the police. Ronnie and Reggie were arrested in May 1968 after careers spanning two decades.

I collected a parking ticket for leaving my Matchless in the wrong place. My grumbles about this at the police sergeant's house were met with, "Don't worry about that; just give it to me." After that, I was able to park where I liked in Croydon and I think I enjoyed my little piece of unearned privilege.

Christmas came and I headed back to The Forest for Mum's cooking and Dad's reassuring company. I went to the Concorde Club with old friends. Here I met a young girl with skinny legs and a very short turquoise blue dress with a silver buckle holding the shoulder straps together. It transpired that she had wanted to meet a tall young man and, when she saw me, decided I qualified. We spent the rest of the evening together and exchanged addresses. I went back to work and Rosie to college in Coventry. She was from Southampton and, like me, visiting home for Christmas.

Rosie and I corresponded and, unsuspecting, I visited her at college. I had no ambition to have a regular girlfriend and, certainly, no intention of taking a wife. I had found a nice rowing club at Putney and there was a lot to explore in London. I felt very self-sufficient. However, we would get together for some weekends, either in Coventry or London. I couldn't have seemed to be much of a catch, still not a high earner and now living in a bed-sitter. However, she seemed to be interested in me, we were comfortable together and I enjoyed her sunny personality.

My accommodation was somewhat limited – just one room and shared facilities. One weekend, with Rosie in residence sharing my single bed, my mother, concerned that I had not corresponded as much as I should, decided to get on the train and bring some home cooking, as a nice surprise, to build up the one she was worrying about and who was floundering in a hostile city. Now mothers, especially those who love their only sons, approach women interested in their precious boys with suspicion. She probably assumed Rosie was some hard city girl with unhealthy motives. It was a pretty uncomfortable collision of people really and not the best way for the two most important women in my life to meet.

I had joined Vesta Rowing Club, a traditional lower Thames club in an old boathouse on the embankment near Putney Bridge. I soon had a seat, the stroke seat, in the Junior Eight. We were coached by the club captain, Ken Bell, an amiable man who loved rowing and inspired us with his enthusiasm. It was here I discovered that rowing spanned the class system and I was rowing with cockney barrow boys and public school educated lawyers. We were focused on the art of rowing and an individual was respected for his commitment and ability. A good model for society; more people should row.

It was great to row on the Tideway, especially on a summer evening when the music of a jazz boat would help us to set a good rhythm.

Ken would cycle along the towpath with a big tin megaphone in one hand, barking out advice. Our coxswain was a 12-year-old lad, too small to see over the crew and would do his best to steer, keeping parallel to the bank. One evening, dinghy sailors were sharing the river with us and Ken had just given the order to "take it up". An eight feels impressive when the power of the crew is applied in unison. We felt like masters of the universe and had not noticed that Ken and bicycle were now lying in a bush.

An unsuspecting wooden dinghy tacked in front of us, but we were all looking the other way, except the cox who, sat behind a crew of big men, couldn't see straight ahead. There was a slight reduction in our speed as our bow struck the transom of the sailing boat. The front of a racing boat is quite fine and ours went right through the dinghy whose sail now caught the wind and veered to one side, snapping off the first three feet or so of our boat. We were now a submarine and went straight to the bottom of the dirty river.

Up until about a year earlier, the Thames had been so dirty that you would have your stomach pumped if it was thought you might have ingested some of its water. We were fine and carried the broken craft the mile or so back to the club. The dinghy was fine and seemed to sail well with our bow sealing the hole.

The gas board was overstaffed and offered only limited opportunity. It only took a few months to get the instrumentation working properly and there didn't seem to be a lot of scope for further personal development. I saw an advertisement for a position as a design engineer for an American industrial gas company called Air Product and Chemicals Inc., based in New Malden. This sounded like the type of work I was looking for and my application was rewarded by an invitation for interview, which I attended. This interesting experience was an hour long grilling during which I was subjected to rapid fire questions on all aspect of process instrumentation by the Chief Instrument Engineer, a small, energetic, aggressive man. As suddenly as the barrage of questions had begun, it ceased. The Chief Engineer stood up and barked at the Personnel Manager, who had been sitting in bewildered silence, "Hire this one" and exited, slamming the door.

I was put to work with Geoff Coster, a dry, amiable Londoner who turned my raw practical knowledge into a skill to specify equipment, design new systems, direct draftsmen and negotiate with vendors.

Rosie came from a respectable working class family; a father with a trade, a wife and three daughters of whom Rosie was the oldest. Like me she had failed the 11+, but there was an educational system in the town and it had been noticed quite quickly that she was bright and she was transferred to Girls Grammar, a respectable school for young ladies.

The family lived in Southampton's western suburb, Freemantle, in a Victorian two up, two down terraced house. By this time it had the extension on the back to provide an inside bathroom and an extra bedroom. It had a best room, only used on Sundays and special occasions and for Father to listen to classical music on the hi-fi system that he had built himself.

On Sundays they went to the Congregational Church. Actually, Rosie's mum went to the Congregational Church while her Dad worked around the house, before a Sunday lunch of roast with two veg. This was followed by a drive to the country in the Morris 8 for a family walk, followed by Sunday tea, followed by Songs of Praise on the telly; all in black and white. Everything was ordered and respectable: black and white.

Auntie Louie, the maiden aunt and family matriarch, was a teacher of geography and the only one in the family to have attained a university degree. As Rosie, sorry Rosemary, had got to the grammar school, she would follow in Auntie Louie's footsteps and, so, she was now at Teacher Training College in Coventry.

It would be difficult for me to find a woman good enough in my mother's eyes; it would be impossible for Rosie to find a suitable man. I didn't know at the time, that on returning home from our first date, Rosie had told her mother that she had met the man she would marry.

It was decided I would visit the home to meet her parents and I arrived, as instructed, after Songs of Praise. I was shown into the front room where Rosie was doing her best to look relaxed, sitting on the floor in front of the artificial log fire. I was not particularly looking forward to this meeting, but I was looking forward to seeing Rosie. After the polite introductions, Rosie noticed something in my trouser pocket.

"What have you got; is it something for me?"

"No, it's nothing," I replied and, in that moment, realised how pleased I was to see her.

"Yes, you have got something in your pocket; I can see it."

Away from home, Rosie was a young lioness stretching her muscles, testing her instincts and looking for a mate – and she had set her sights. At home she was a kitten, still unsteady on her feet and naively testing the world, expecting the parental rebuke that often came.

Her mother took an interest; perhaps it was a present for her? And then, realising it was not, she left the room abruptly, muttering about controlling oneself. I had not impressed on my first attempt.

This did strain Rosie's relationship, already fragile, with her parents. She didn't want to be a teacher and wasn't enjoying the course at Coventry, but didn't know how to explain this at home. She had never really wanted to be a teacher and, now she had experienced a teaching practice with live children, she definitely knew it was not for her.

We continued to meet at weekends and, on one of her visits to London, we visited her maternal grandmother who lived in Battersea, also in a Victorian terraced house. I was wearing a jumper beautifully knitted by my mother, with a complicated pattern in a band around the chest.

Grandma admired it and, in what I thought was an obvious joke, I replied, "Yes, I knitted it myself; there is not much for a young man living alone in London to do in the evenings."

I thought no more about this until Rosie reported the scolding from her mother, when she had heard from her mother about the wonderful homecraft skills of Rosemary's boyfriend.

How had it come to this? The daughter who would earn family pecking order points for her mother, fallen to the depths of dating and intending to marry, a motorcyclist with an erection who lied to old ladies!

I was living a sort of double-think life at this time. I had not been looking for a wife; I was still looking for adventure and I had not noticed that this relationship was growing increasingly serious. The British Antarctic Survey was recruiting engineers. Now that sounded like an adventure so I applied. They agreed they would take me; I would be trained as a meteorologist, but I would have to wait for the Antarctic thaw that would allow the John Biscoe in next season. The Antarctic was put on ice and I returned to my routine.

Christmas came round again and somehow, without me noticing, Rosie and I had become engaged. Predictably, her parents were not thrilled and planning for a wedding became very complicated and difficult. At first, more to keep the peace than out of commitment, Rosie had said she would complete her course at Coventry.

Dad wrote me a letter, dated 21 October 1969, with the line, "… and I am very happy about your engagement. She is a fine girl and I think you are a very lucky fellow. What I am sure of is that when you meet the right person, just give and take a little and hang on with both hands because it's the very best thing that you can get out of life." Dad was a good judge of character. I hung on with both hands and found he was right.

I had begun to think about where we might live. It was very hard to find a rented flat in the London area; there were plenty of advertisements in the evening papers but the place was always gone by the time the paper came out. My dad was resourceful; what would he do? Obvious; I would walk every street that looked as though its houses were big enough to have been converted to flats and knock on every door until I found a vacancy. I started in Homersham Road, Norbiton and knocked on the first promising door.

"No, this is a house, no flats, but the woman three doors' down on the other side has just converted her top floor and I think it will be up for rent soon."

I went straight to Number 68 where Mrs Darlison confirmed that she would be looking for a tenant; £7 a week. I paid a deposit and moved in a month later.

Relationships were not any better in Freemantle and unnecessary complications were still being invented. Rosie was not enjoying her teacher training and time at home became uncomfortable for her to the extent that we could not see the benefit of continuing in that mode. I went to see the bishop and bought a special licence. We would be able to be married within two weeks in my parish church in Exbury.

Roger – with whom I shared a deep and lasting bond, forged at the work bench of the Apprentice Training Centre – had met Marion, whom he had renamed "Maz" to make her more modern and they had formed a different sort of deep and lasting bond that had led to them marrying a few months earlier.

By now our relationship with Rosie's parents had become fragile and, concerned that she would have a distressing time at home, I suggested that she move into the flat in Norbiton with me and she agreed.

The next week was the company dinner-dance. At that time the tradition was to book the Great Room of Grosvenor House Hotel and, that year, Rosie and I were able to attend. This was a splendid black tie affair with dancing to Sidney Lipton and his Band and a display by the musicians of the Coldstream Guards who marched in, in full regalia.

We were pleased to see an 8ft. x 6ft. oil painting in the entrance hall of the hotel, of the pre-war ice rink that had been my dad's workplace those years ago. I couldn't make dad out in the characters circulating on the ice, but I'm sure he was there.

On Friday 30 January 1970, the day before our wedding, we travelled to the New Forest. I dropped Rosie off with Roger and Maz. We had intended that Rosie would wear a smart suit for the wedding, there having been no time to arrange a bridal gown and, anyway, we had not saved any money for the occasion. However, another recently married friend, Beverley, had a dress only worn once and offered it. Rosie had tried it on and it was a perfect fit.

It was never clear how it happened, but our parents had got together and decided to help make the day a success. Rosie's dad agreed to give her away at the church and the families would be invited.

Rather in the manner of the bridal dress, two bridesmaids' dresses materialised that fitted Rosie's little sister and my cousin. My partner in poaching (*not* strawberry stealing) crime, Tom, had agreed to be my best man. This seemed to be appropriate as he had been my partner in totty hunting the night I met Rosie at the Concord Club.

Rosie, Maz and Beverley had a nice meal and an early night. Roger and I went out with Tom and a few friends and shared the ritual that young men share in as many of the New Forest's pubs as we could manage and had a late night.

Tom was an unenthusiastic Best Man, but he did get me to the church on time, stopping as necessary to allow me to vomit up the last of the previous evening's excesses.

Our friends and families seemed to be free on that day, 31 January. The day was cold but Rosie looked as radiant and lovely as any bride and the thaw that had begun in the relationship with her parents warmed further. I don't think anyone noticed that it was a second-hand wedding in the old stone Church of St. Katherine, deep in the New Forest, where Rothchilds marry.

Good, resourceful Mum had booked the Esso club for the reception, organised flowers, cake and just about everything else. I found the receipts in Mum's lifetime collection of paper: reception, £55 11s 11d; flowers, £10 1s 6d; cake, £8 (she would have made that, but there was not enough time for the requisite amount of alcohol to soak in to one of Mum's fruit cakes). Dad's job had been to drive around the New Forest pubs collecting up my wallet, clothes and belongings abandoned on the drunken evening before the wedding day.

After a short honeymoon in Swanage, we moved into our first home – officially. The John Biscoe had sailed without me.

Rosie got a job in the Decca Radar technical library and I continued at Air Products until a colleague on assignment from the head office in Pennsylvania came to help out for a few months. He was an Irish American and it turned out that he was on a mission: he planned to start his own business in Ireland where he saw an opportunity to bring his knowledge of modern industrial instrumentation to a country where the only industry was a few dairies and a Guinness factory, but that was just beginning to receive investment in new industries. He would need someone to help him so the business could earn some income while he made connections and searched out opportunities.

Well, this sounded like an adventure that Rosie and I could undertake together. No matter that she was now pregnant; they have babies in Ireland don't they?

We would be based in Cork where a new pharmaceutical plant to manufacture citric acid was being built and there was an opportunity for us to provide consultancy in instrumentation. Actually, I would work as their instrument engineer and accept completed systems from the engineering contractor as they were commissioned. This was exactly what the business needed.

112

Chapter 11

Cork

It never snows in Cork, located almost at the south-west corner of the British Isles and cosseted by the Gulf Stream. Plenty of that gentle precipitation between mist and rain. "It's-a-fine-soft-morning-so-it-is" kind of rain.

Speech in Cork has an accent that is soft like its weather; coloured by a rhythm borrowed from the people a ferry ride away in Wales and made Irish again by its gentle phrases and Gaelic abandoned aitches.

Rosie woke me gently at around three in the morning and, as I opened my eyes, she said calmly "The contractions have started."

"Not due for another week," I replied and turned over.

Again, a bit more insistently this time, followed by a quick intake of breath.

Well, I had never done this before but I am an engineer and it is just a mechanical process that can easily be managed with a little analysis, some calculation and a bit of planning. I timed the contractions over the next two hours and, yes, they were getting closer together. My graph revealed that the baby would arrive at 10.20am, so I determined we would go to Saint Finbarr's just after 8am to give us time for registration and getting comfortable.

Saint Finbarr's was an old hospital with grey, stern walls. We should have been suspicious when the doctor had said, "What classes? You just push when you're told to." That had been a couple of months earlier, just after we arrived on the Emerald Isle.

"You can leave now," said the nun at the desk. "You've done your part and you should leave now."

She was pleasant enough, but with an authority that is delegated directly from the Prefect for the Congregation for the Doctrine of the Faith – once known as the Inquisition.

113

If there was any thought of resistance it was defeated, finally, by that scent of purity and power that all nuns carry: carbolic soap.

There's not much to do in Cork on Christmas Day, especially if you're not a catholic. So I walked through the city. It was very quaint. Oliver Plunkett Street, Grand Parade, The English Market (the tripe and drisheen stalls and those that sell crubeens all closed up) and along the banks of the Lee past the dormant rowing clubs (good Catholics don't row on Christmas Day).

I'll go back and see how things are going; the baby will have arrived by now I thought.

The sentinel had changed but the message had not.

"No, nothing has happened."

This nun, however, had weakness and it was Christmas after all.

"You may have a quick word," she conceded.

Rosie looked very comfortable in the high metal bed.

"Oh no, nothing has happened and the Christmas dinner was wonderful, especially as someone else cooked it."

You can interrupt labour for a Christmas dinner. There was a lot I didn't know about childbirth.

My expulsion soon followed and I found myself back on the street. I hadn't planned for this. Back by the river and now snow started to fall, just gentle, sparse flakes; a very soft kind of snow, but it was snow. If it is possible to be in a place with absolutely no sound, this was that place. No people, no traffic, no wind, no bird sound. No sound. I walked and thought and reflected on my situation. Was I grateful to the girl who would bear me a child or resentful of the undisciplined person who had declined to follow my graph? I was hungry, cold and lonely, but on the edge of one of life's great experiences. Shame I wouldn't be there, but I had done my part.

A further, fruitless visit to the grey walls and another brief consultation.

"The contractions have started again," I was advised. And reminded, "This is no place for a husband." I went for another walk. Eventually, and it was half an hour past Christmas now, I was allowed in to see mother and baby. They were both ready for sleep.

On my return in the morning, Rosie and baby had plimmed up nicely; in fact the new mother looked positively radiant as she suckled the infant.

"Is it a boy or a child?" enquired the guest in the next room, using one of those gentle Cork phrases.

It was a boy. I had a son.

We named him Finbarr.

The telegram was still the artery of communication on special occasions in 1970. Back in England my parents had passed the news of our first child and a message arrived from friends in The New Forest, Roger and Maz. It was a distillation of the rounded laconic speech of rural Hampshire and those abandoned aitches of Cork. "Thrust it was born in a manger" said the pasted words on the stiff paper – the operator's interpretation of Roger's reliable humour.

We had been living in Cork, well Monkstown actually, on the very edge of Cork harbour, for three months. Our home was a flat on the third floor of a house originally built by the British Admiralty, looking across a broad sweep of the harbour approach. The road runs along the water's edge from Cork, through Douglas, Passage West, Glenbrook, Monkstown and Ringaskiddy. The names of the villages, like the people and like the weather, are soft and friendly.

It was comfortable when these open, warm people welcomed us home from St. Finbarr's with our proud addition; and gave us clothes and toys for the baby.

115

"He's a dote," a woman would say.

A man would press a small coin into the baby's hand and nod approvingly at the mother.

This was a time of heightened conflict in Northern Ireland and there seemed to be fewer men around in Passage West on the weekends before the Monday papers reported "activity" in the North.

Some days I would read reports of the same incidents in The Irish Times and the Daily Telegraph and it was very disappointing to see the extent to which "news" was distorted. It is wonderful, essential even, to have a free press, but it would be so much more valuable to society if this was more responsible and worked harder to communicate a fair picture of events. In a democracy people should be free to decide how to vote, but freedom is truncated if we are fed distorted or partisan data. I really wonder if this misleading of the electorate damages democracy to the extent that some then feel violence to be the only way to communicate their views.

A rubber bullet was a favourite trophy for the mantelpiece in a Cork home. I suppose they remembered the burning of Cork and murder of its mayor in 1920 by The Black and Tans. Perhaps they read the Irish Times or listened to their priests while people in England read the Telegraph and felt equally hostile towards them.

We experienced only warmth and encouragement from the people of that friendly country. It was a good place to be and, although we would have valued family contact at that time, we enjoyed growing together as a family; Rosie, Finbarr and I depending on each other. Rosie was just 21 and I, 24.

We had a handed down copy of Dr. Spock's book, Baby and Child Care. One day at lunchtime I nipped home from work to see my family, to find the novice mother with baby on one arm, a plastic bath before them and the book in the other hand.

We were not trained or equipped for this role but we were conscientious. This must happen to all new parents and it happened to us. We prepared the small bedroom as a nursery and placed the baby in his crib the first night. It seemed like a good arrangement and we were proud that we had made responsible provision for our new offspring. Of course it was only minutes before Rosie went to check he was "still breathing". Then it was my turn. We repeated this at short intervals before bringing baby and crib into our room, then moving it closer, then right up to the side of the bed. It was a lovely, fulfilling, but worrying experience to be in charge of a new life.

I was not earning a lot of money but we lived comfortably enough. Our flat was warm and clean and beautifully located. Our transport was a clapped out minivan I had bought cheaply from a colleague before we left England. I spent a lot of time under that van, coaxing it into a few more miles of service. This was usually in the gutter of the side road near the flat and with the fine, soft weather of Cork, usually lying in running rain water. There wasn't quite enough money to buy all the equipment we might have liked for the baby and, for our first trip home to the New Forest, he was transported in the bottom drawer from our second-hand chest.

Our flat was in a beautiful location and with a view that changed with the weather and the ships that passed through to Cobh and Cork. This was a world away from the south-east of England with its traffic, its bustle, its crowds, but at this time in our lives the space, the views and the tranquillity of Monkstown on the edge of Cork Harbour did very nicely.

It was an impressive sight when the fleet of the Crosshaven Yacht Club's annual race was powering up the channel with spinnakers full, running before the wind and straight towards our living room.

The yacht club claims to be the oldest in the world and is properly named "The Royal Cork Yacht Club". It was King William IV, a King of England and Ireland, who granted the "Royal" title of which the patrons are now so proud.

In May every year there was an activity in Monkstown that was shared in the community. A boy would run up the road and past our front door, past all the front doors, shouting, "The mackerel are coming! The mackerel are coming!" I had been warned to have a fishing rod with spinner ready and, on hearing the boy's invitation in our first June, I ran down the stairs, picked up the rod that had been loaded and ready, just inside the front door, crossed the road that carried one car an hour in its most busy period and onto the little wooden jetty that seemed to be there for this very purpose. In a moment, there were men with fishing rods all up and down the river. The water was boiling as the muscular mackerel harassed the whitebait that fled up the estuary. Three casts – three mackerel for dinner.

There's lots of water in Ireland and, if you are a rower, this is an invitation that you have to accept. There were three rowing clubs in Cork. I joined Lee, on a straight part of the river about a mile below the city centre. They immediately made me welcome and put me in their men's eight. We trained regularly and raced up and down southern Ireland on rivers, lakes and estuaries. Rowing is a community activity. The rowing club had social evenings for the families of members and these were grand affairs. Many would volunteer to do their party piece to entertain the gathering; there was excellent singing and storytelling.

Jim Riordan would put aside his Cork accent and become a Lancashire man to recite Stanley Holloway's monologue about the unfortunate Albert with 'is 'orse's 'ead 'andle. It was expected of you to have a party piece for such occasions.

118

For all their probity and formality, these good people thought nothing of giving Guinness to the young children – and Finbarr seemed to enjoy it.

Regatta days were great fun in Ireland; Rosie, Finbarr and I would be there with the families of the other rowers, Finbarr enjoying the constant attention of the girls and mums. An essential piece of rowing equipment that always went with us was an old copper – an electrically heated drum for boiling clothes. A power source would be found and the boiler filled with water and crubeens and switched on, at a low heat. It would simmer all day and, when the racing was over, we all tucked in. Crubeens are pigs' trotters and they have a lovely sweet, chewy taste – just the job with a glass of Guinness after a good day out.

The mother of Jim Riordan the coxswain died. I mumbled my condolences and thought that was the end of it. Although I got on well with Jim we were not especially close and I hadn't known his mother. I was surprised when I was detailed by the club captain to come to the church for the funeral and then to join the procession and the wake. It seemed that the tradition was that you had to attend a funeral if you knew a relative of the deceased. That's how they have such a fine turnout for funerals in Cork.

The captain of Lee Rowing club was Mr. Twomey – known as "Mr. Twomey"; I don't know if he had a Christian name. He was a gentle, inspirational man, around 65-years-old when I rowed with Lee, who coached us from the coxwain's seat in overcoat and trilby hat! People here managed to combine warmth and formality at the same time; it was part of the charm of our Cork experience.

Mr Twomey went to 6am mass every morning.

I asked him, "Mr. Twomey, you spend a lot of time going to mass; are you sure there is anyone listening?"

He replied sincerely, "No, I'm not, but I'm not going to take any chances with my immortal soul."

This is known by students of philosophy as *Pascal's Wager*. Blaise Pascal was a 16th century polymath: mathematician, scientist and philosopher. I don't know whether Mr. Twomey studied philosophy, but he gave the impression that he didn't need to.

Mr. Twomey's philosophy was no bad thing. He was a man of character who could be relied upon. He seemed to me to be a man who had made a full contribution in his professional life and in his private life; he was content with the world, and without being complacent, with himself. Indeed, the people of Cork never seemed complacent. To any comment about a plan for the future, even for tomorrow, was appended a cheerful, "God willing," and any satisfactory news was endorsed with "Thanks be to God."

Religion was present in everyday language, usually in a natural and sincere way, although there seemed to be some clever double thinking practised if adherence to the faith interfered too much in practical matters. If I needed to make a business trip to the UK, as I occasionally did, my team at the citric acid plant would ask me to buy a Playboy magazine for them. Such things were not available in the republic at that time. I would smuggle the magazine into the country and pass it to one of the men who would take it home to read and then pass it on. On one occasion, I was approached by one of them: "Patrick has had the magazine rather a long time and I would like my turn". Patrick was a middle aged man and you might have thought, master of his house, but had concealed the illegal and subversive publication from his wife by hiding it under the fridge. She had washed the floor and the magazine was ruined. The others would have to wait for my next trip.

A little mischievously, I asked Patrick, "Did you enjoy your reading?"

"Oh yes, t'anks a lot."

"Well, Patrick, what are you going to tell the priest on Sunday, when you go to confession?"

Patrick thought for a few moments. "Sure, an' and I didn't enjoy it t'at much."

This was a neat way of avoiding unnecessary stress.

A bonus for Catholics is the army of saints available to help in any situation and you could sometimes hear women swapping saints. "I lost my watch but found it after praying to St. Anthony." There was St. Sergius for making a cake rise, or the heavy weights like St. Peter for marital difficulties. I suppose this might be called "practical Catholicism" and what is wrong with it? If prayer is a way of focusing the mind and being reminded that there is a universe far more important than the individual and, if things get done, then prayer is surely good.

About 5% of the population of Eire were Protestants – Anglicans – and adherents of the Church of Ireland. One of the staff in my department was a protestant. Not surprisingly, he had a Catholic girlfriend. They wanted to marry and their families were reasonably comfortable with the idea of a "mixed marriage", as such a union was referred to in Eire. Mixed marriage is a term we don't hear today in England, but then it was used to describe a marriage between people of different races; in Ireland it referred to different religions.

They went to see the girl's priest who counselled them to wait a year and then see how they felt. A year passed and they went back to the priest who instructed them to wait for another year. I don't know whether they ever married. Such was the power of the Catholic Church over its people in that place at that time and how far it had drifted from the ideals of the man who taught that leadership is service. It is easy to understand how thoughts on any subject, the "English Occupation", for example, could be influenced.

The business was developing satisfactorily; my work on the pharmaceutical plant covered the overheads and my partner scoured the country for new opportunities. He secured the agencies for a number of international brands in the process instrumentation and related fields, but all his successes were for the sale of equipment rather than engineering opportunities.

I saw my future as an engineer, not a salesman and Rosie and I decided to return to the UK. This was not good timing. In America they were in a decade of strikes and its economy was flagging. When America catches a cold, Europe sneezes. At home, the economy had not been strong under Harold Wilson's Labour government, but when Ted Heath won the general election in 1971 and took on the unions – unsuccessfully as it transpired – the economy declined further.

It had been foolish to put myself out of work and it was very uncomfortable with a family to support. There seemed to be no opportunities, but after only about three weeks an offer came from the pharmaceutical company and I joined their staff back in Cork.

Chapter 12

Bloody Sunday

Back in Cork we found rented accommodation in Glenbrook, not far from our British Admiralty flat in Monkstown. It was while we were in Glenbrook that I was reminded I had an allergy to citric acid – not the best thing for someone working on a plant producing the stuff. I suppose I was absorbing the acid and it eventually built up to the point that I had a sudden major reaction. I came out in a rash covering every part of my body that was so irritating that I thought I would go mad. By 9pm one evening, I couldn't stand it any longer and drove to the house of Dr. Barry. Jerome Francis Barry was a flamboyant young doctor with a shock of red hair. As he opened his door - and even before I stepped into the light – he diagnosed a severe allergic reaction.

"Not to worry; I'll give you an injection."

He fumbled around under the stairs muttering that he was sure he had some samples he could use. He gave up the search and invited me to follow him to his surgery where there was more fumbling on the chaotic desk and overloaded bookshelves.

"Ah, here it is," he said at last.

He injected the contents of one phial, then another, just to be sure. Then he read the instructions. "Do not drive or operate machinery after using this medication" was the warning.

"As you're driving, you'd better hurry," he advised.

I was now eight miles from home with an unfenced road on the harbour's edge to negotiate. I took Dr. Barry's advice and hurried. I got home and, immediately on opening the door, passed out. I slept soundly for at least eight hours after which I awoke feeling fine.

This was the same Dr. Barry whom I had called when we were in the Admiralty flat. Our neighbour, Tony had woken us around two in the morning.

"Sorry to wake you," he said apologetically.

He looked ill.

"I feel dizzy, I've got palpitations and I'm worried I might be having a heart attack."

We sat him down while I called the doctor.

"Sorry to trouble you Dr. Barry; my neighbour feels dizzy, has got palpitations and is worried he might be having a heart attack."

"Ah, sure an' there's a lot of that about," he said groggily before putting down the receiver.

We gave Tony some water and watched him for a while. He survived the night. Dr. Barry was right.

We got used to the doctor's casual attitude and came to appreciate his candour. When I later contracted viral pneumonia and was very unwell, he called to examine me. When I asked him for his diagnosis, he said, "We'll call it TB for now and work from there."

I felt at home in Cork; perhaps the experiences of my grandmother's line had been passed subliminally to me through my mother who had many Irish characteristics (stoicism, superstition, generosity...) even though she had not visited the country before visiting us.

We had parachuted into Cork, not of that community, not sharing their traditions, or understanding what was important to them; but they took us in and allowed us to join in their lives. Communities all over the world are like this in rural places and small towns. I think it's different in big cities.

I developed a passable Cork accent. I don't know whether I did this to avoid being treated as a tourist, to be more easily understood, or just because I wanted to be absorbed into the community.

It wasn't, as you might expect, to avoid anti-British feeling: there was never any of that at a personal level. Sometimes I would hear a negative comment about the English – always the "English" and not "British" – but this would quickly be followed by "But not you; we've nothing against you."

The Irish sense of humour is much more subtle than I realised before I lived in Ireland. The English like to laugh at the stupidity of the Irish, but this is turned cleverly in such a way that you can't be sure who the joke is on. I witnessed many examples of this. One was when a colleague, Donal O'Riordan, was making a call to England to a number we often used: Redhill 65000. It became apparent that he had reached the wrong number when the English voice replied that Redhill 65001 was connected. In his broadest Cork accent, Donal said "Sure, an' you must be next door; would you mind just popping round with a message?"

The purring of the disconnected line was immediately heard and Donal smiled in the confidence that someone in England was now being told, "Do you know what a stupid Irishman on the phone just said to me?"

You could never be sure when the joke was on you.

When the visitors came - Rosie's parents and my parents - it was the opportunity and excuse to explore southern Ireland. Even close to Cork city, there was almost no traffic on the roads and good roads too; a government sponsored make-work programme was to employ people improving roads. These were no motorways but wide, well surfaced single carriageway roads. Some of them seemed excessively large for their traffic duty, but I guess their main purpose was to provide employment.

We went to West Cork there were beaches of white sand that stretched for miles and you could have to yourself; there were deserted hills and peat bogs, verdant valleys and lush woodlands.

A magic spot we liked was Gougane Barra, west of Macroom in County Cork, where the River Lee rises. It is a steep sided valley hung with trees and, each time we visited, it was shrouded in mist that rolls gently down nature's green walls to a still, glassy lake that has a small island on which is built a stone chapel. This was originally the hermitage of St. Finbarr, founder and first bishop of Cork in the sixth century. In England this would be the lake from which Guinevere's hand offering Excalibur to the young Arthur would emerge as an ethereal breeze disturbed its otherwise placid surface. In Ireland it is a haven of tranquillity where saints purge their souls and achieve communion with creation.

In Glengarriff, near the head of Bantry Bay, the mist again provided the atmosphere as we made the short crossing in a small boat to Garnish Ireland where the garden of Ilnacullin with lily pond, mock temple and ornamental clock tower is protected by a perimeter of trees and illuminated by rhododendrons, flowering shrubs and perennials. It was built early in the twentieth century, just to take advantage of the Gulf Stream's warmth and the Emerald Isle's misty irrigation and for no other reason than to be a pleasant place.

We stayed at a hotel in the town of Glengarriff where we enjoyed a good, simple meal, relaxed with a few drinks and chatted to the landlord who seemed intelligent and well informed. Fairly late in the evening, a rustic, farmer type burst into the bar and demanded a Paddy's. This was provided, then another and the landlord listened with reverence to the farmer's tale.

"It's happened again. 'e stands at the foot of me bed and berates me; I can't stand it anymore. 'e was bad enough when 'e was alive but now…"

When the farmer had received sufficient consolation – and whiskey ("whiskey" has an 'e' in Ireland) - he left, a little less abruptly than he had entered.

As we admired the landlord for his sympathy and tact in dealing with the distressed and fanciful customer, we expected him to say something to the effect that the irrational and superstitious behaviour we had witnessed was the unfortunate product of a feeble mind.

What he actually said was, "Sure, an' t'at's a terrible t'ing to happen to a fella, still getting nightly visits from his neighbour and him dead these two years. Of course they didn't get along at all, at all."

You could never be sure...

The Irish like to leave room in life for a little mystery and colour this with a tincture of superstition. In the rest of the world, theists and atheists, at intervals, have their (unnecessary) arguments about the existence of God. In Ireland the philosophy about anything is, "If it makes life better, it's true enough".

Rosie, Finbarr and I were walking on the Old Head of Kinsale, not far from Cork, which is an idyllic beautiful spot number 37 (not in order of idyll or beauty, just one of hundreds of such places in Eire). This was the Titanic's last view of Europe in 1912 and it had probably not changed in the intervening years. Sadly, in the 1990s when Eire was enjoying its Celtic Tiger years, the Old Head was made into a golf course. A scar is most distressing when it destroys great beauty.

On that day the breeze ruffled the seed-heads of the grass against the deep blue-green of the Atlantic and occasionally brought a wisp of mist towards and past us. Here and there were hummocks of grass to break up the uniformity of the otherwise smoothly carpeted headland. I glanced over my shoulder and, out of the corner of my eye, spotted my first leprechaun, traditionally dressed, sat on a hummock. I turned to get Rosie's attention, but when we looked back he was there no more.

Now, you might think this is fanciful, but I think the leprechaun improved my day and just knowing he is out there somewhere adds a little mystery and colour to life.

Even on the days after Sunday, 30 January 1972, people continued to be warm and friendly towards us. The Paras had opened fire and people had died. All the tensions of the long, bloody history that was blamed on the English were inflamed. There was only one perspective reported in the newspapers. How could people not be angry? But, again, there was no personal animosity. We were all shocked and many of the British living in Cork went to mass the following Sunday, just to show respect. I attended the little church in Ringaskiddy, where the priest, alone, was cool towards me.

An English couple who helped us to acclimatise when we first arrived, and with whom we became friends, were the Tubbys: Maureen and John. John managed the Cork office of the Gestetner company. From time to time, John would have a visit from an activist.

"Mr. Tubby, sir, we're sorry to trouble you but we're goin' to need to blow up your office."

As an English company in Cork, Gestetner, needed to be blown up occasionally. John would withdraw his staff and important papers to a safe distance and a modest incendiary bomb would be detonated – just enough to need the fire service and to blacken the front of the shop. It was all very polite and not "personal".

One side effect of cultivating a local accent - and the people of Cork, especially from south of the river, could be difficult to understand - was that I sometimes needed to translate what was being said by Cogan the electrician, or other sing-songy, fast-talking local, for Irish visitors from outside Cork.

We bought a house closer to Cork city in a district called Beaumont. It cost us £7200, which was probably about 10% more than a similar house in Surrey. It was in a pleasant residential area, semi-detached and quite well built in the style of newer houses in Ireland: rendered elevations

128

painted white. There was a garage and workshop and a reasonably large garden.

We enjoyed making Irish friends, but inevitably ex-patriots tended to gravitate together. We had met the Collins' when they gave up the flat we rented in Monkstown. Peter Collins had worked for Pfizer at their UK facility in Sandwich, Kent and now also worked at the citric acid plant. A visit to their house was a welcome oasis of middle class Englishness. Sue was an excellent cook and host and Peter was always amiable. This was to gradually build into a lifelong friendship and our children adopted "Auntie Sue and Uncle Peter".

My job was now Instrument Engineer, Pfizer, Ringaskiddy. I was the instrument engineer responsible for the instrument maintenance department. At the age of 24, they had a lot of confidence in me.

There were almost no technicians in Ireland with relevant experience. I recruited twelve men with various sorts of technical training and set about teaching them what they would need to know about process instrumentation. I wrote the training course and delivered it at intervals as new people were hired. I provisioned the stores, planned the work and provided technical supervision. When the plant was "debottlenecked", I designed the new systems. I had complete freedom and control.

Another Irish joke, at least I think it was – you could never be sure – from the Irish Dunlop factory. I bought Wellington boots for the stores and, when they arrived, there was an "R" embossed on the right boot and "L" on the left.

The most suitable recruits came from the Royal Airforce. These were Irishmen who had served around 12 years in the RAF and were trained aircraft artificers. Next best were those from the Irish Airforce. Then there were those who had worked in large scale dairies, or creameries, as they were known.

The men were reluctant to keep asking me for advice. One device they used to determine whether an instrument was beyond repair was to place it in the waste bin in the workshop, carefully arranged so I would see it when I entered. As programmed, I would declare "You can't throw this away." They would apologise and set about dismantling it for overhaul.

Most of the employees had no experience of work in a disciplined multi-national company and came from a culture in which timekeeping was casual. I tried to explain to James O'Shaugnessy that he was 20 minutes or so late for work every day and would he please come to work on time at 8 o'clock.

"Sure, an' I wasn't late this morning, I particularly checked the clock on The Custom House and it said 8 o'clock."

That sounded fine, but The Custom House was 10 miles away in Cork city.

At the first annual shutdown I planned overhaul of all the equipment that couldn't be easily isolated with the plant running. To help the team through their first shutdown, I produced detailed work sheets and checklists for each job. It was James O'Shaugnessy who had the task of overhauling the air driers. His sheet detailed the work – go to the drier in Building 3 – isolate the drier by closing valves V132, 133, 146 and tag the valves – depressurise – etc. – remove the non-return valves and inspect the seats – and so on.

When we came to re-commission the equipment, the air drier in Building 3 was not working; there was leakage somewhere. I went through the operation with James, checked that he had added new grease to the four-way valve and I added just a little more (too much would get into the dry air). I went through James' work sheet step-by-step. Yes, he had done everything. The only explanation I could think of was a leaking non-return valve, but his checklist showed that he had "dismantled and inspected". I took out the valves and it was plain that the seats were seriously worn and would definitely leak.

"Sure, an' I noticed that," said James confidently.

"But you didn't replace the seats, James."

"It didn't say 'replace the seats' on the sheet," he replied innocently.

You could never be sure...

It had been a struggle to buy the house in Beaumont, but we were keen to own our own home to complete our family life.

Christmas came and Finbarr had his first birthday. We bought him Lego, the original small bricks; the only type available at that time. I enjoyed playing with my son and his Lego. Truthfully, I enjoyed playing with the Lego while my son amused himself.

We had bought the house from an enthusiastic but incompetent do-it-yourselfer. One of his masterpieces had been to glue red Formica directly on to the kitchen walls. We had little money but a lot of energy and we were able to strip it off and reuse the timber from the shaky cabinets to make new cabinets. The doors of the new cabinets and work surfaces were covered with the salvaged Formica. We thought it looked pretty good and we went on to strip unsuitable and badly applied paint around the house until we got things into, what we felt, was good order.

I dug a vegetable patch and planted it – just like my father had done each time he had a new garden. Our crops, especially the greens, grew rampantly in the virgin soil and soft Cork climate and we didn't buy vegetables that year. I resolved that we would be vegetable self-sufficient for a full 12 months. We managed it, but this necessitated living on curly kale for about four months. We ate a lot of colcannon which is a cork favourite, a mixture of mashed potato, curly kale and onion.

Rosie was "with child" again. This was straightforward and the baby was born in St. Finbarr's Hospital – without the help of the husband ("This is no place for a husband") – in May. She was a beautiful girl in need of an Irish name. We liked Ciara, but thought the Gaelic spelling might be difficult for English relatives and we anglicised it to Kiera.

Now two sets of nappies to be rinsed, sanitised with Milton solution and hand washed; we had not yet aspired to a washing machine. Rosie didn't complain. I think we both worked pretty hard.

The radiator boiled and the minivan finally expired. We needed another car and the gracious Mr. Twomey of the rowing club was changing his immaculate Wolseley 1660 for a new Triumph. Even though the price was very reasonable, it was more than we could really afford. However, we thought it was too good to miss and I took a loan from The Bank of Ireland. I never told my parents I had borrowed money!

Rosie said she felt unwell and she was coughing in a rattley, congested way, producing mucus with what appeared to be blood in it. Then it was only hours before she was so weak that I had to carry her up to bed. Her condition deteriorated further; she had a high temperature and became delirious and was drifting in and out of consciousness. I was worried. I called Dr. Barry who came at once. He examined Rosie and looked concerned.

"She's quite ill," he agreed.

"I'll try this," he said as he sifted the contents of his bag and produced a phial.

I had heard this from Dr. Barry before, but urgent action was needed, I could see that.

We watched her for a while, but he seemed to expect a more rapid response.

"I think we'll have to hit this hard," he said gravely and got out what appeared to be a bigger syringe. He loaded it and pumped its contents into Rosie's arm. I can't remember how long it was, but it seemed to take effect very quickly. She opened her eyes and smiled. After a short sleep, she was back with me - back in the land of the living.

"Thanks be to God," I heard myself say, just like Mr. Twoomey or Patrick or...

Many years later, Finbarr ("Finny") and Kiera, now young adults, visited Cork. They tried to find the house where we had lived in Beaumont. They knocked on a door and were invited in for tea and cakes by a welcoming family. They did not determine whether they had found the right house, but they received a taste of the warmth of Cork people.

Finny and Kiera also visited Lee Rowing Club with a grainy old black-and-white photograph of a rowing crew posing with the Goff Shield they had just won at Waterford Regatta.

At the top of the stairs, over the boathouse, they approached a smallish man sat at the rowing club bar.

"Excuse us," they said tentatively, "We are visiting and wondered whether anyone here might know any of the people in this photo."

The young men in the picture were wearing Lee racing kit alright and, "Yes, this is Charlie Fitzgerald, this Jim Fitzpatrick and here is John Donovan..." He seemed to know them all.

Finny and Kiera were surprised; they had been sceptical about my heroic rowing stories from Ireland and had not expected to get much response.

"That's amazing," they chimed in unison, "How did you know all this?"

"Well, that one there is me, Jim Riordan – I was the cox."

"And were they any good, this crew of our dad's?"

"No, not really, but with some good coxing, they managed to win a few races."

Not really! We had won nearly every race we entered in 1971, on the rivers, lakes and estuaries of Ireland from Cork to Limerick, to Dublin, to Waterford.

We had enjoyed particular rivalry with Trinity College, Dublin Boat Club that year. By the time Waterford Regatta came round they were fed up with us beating them and they arrived with a new boat and half the crew replaced. As usual we were late at the start and slow to begin the race. Trinity must have thought their strategy was paying off and the usual psychology in rowing is: get a lead then dominate the opposition. However, we had just got into the habit of winning races and there was a stubbornness about our crew that didn't allow for not winning. We rowed them down, they panicked and we passed them to win the Goff Shield.

The psychology of crew rowing is subtle: if just one crew member is suspected of less than full commitment, then the doubts of the others become enough to damage the willpower needed to push through the pain barrier in the harder moments of the race.

I was encouraged after the race, to overhear members of Trinity talking: "They're canny these Cork men..." I wasn't a real Cork man, but I realised I felt good about being included as one; they are good people with character.

The job was going quite well and I had gained fantastic experience, but it started to become apparent that the senior jobs would go to Irish nationals as the British and American staff from the start-up team gradually withdrew. When an offer came to return to Air Products, whose business was picking up, we decided to take it. This was 1973.

Chapter 13

Big Wide World

British Industry had enjoyed a period of growth in the 50s and 60s, stimulated by the investment of the post-war Labour government, but outmoded practices and antagonistic labour relations had not been addressed. By the 70s, however, other countries were developing and modernising their industries faster than Britain where we were stuck in a downward spiral of under-investment, distrust between managers and workers, ineffective management and militant unions. This malaise became known as the British Disease and it gave Britain the lowest productivity of any industrialised country, even Italy.

In 1973, Conservative Prime Minister, Edward Heath, took us into the EEC and membership further exposed Britain's lack of competitiveness; living standards declined and industrial strife brought industry to a near stand-still. We had a 50 mph speed limit, a three day week, miners' strike and a "winter of discontent". In 1974, Ted Heath asked "Who governs Britain?" When he went to the country, he found out that it wasn't him.

Working for American owned companies was becoming a habit for me, but with well run British companies now hard to find, it was a good compromise and Air Products had a positive ethos (although I discovered that "ethos" is not a word used by Americans and they are completely unable to pronounce it. The language differences were to be an enduring source of amusement for both British and American colleagues over the years).

We bought a house in Surrey; in Wilcot Gardens, Bisley. This was painful financially; it cost nearly twice as much as we had sold the Beaumont house for and the mortgage interest rate was 12%.

The economy was in a poor condition, but I was fortunate to have skills in current demand and to be welcomed back by a company successful in international business. The house was comfortable though and pleasantly situated at the end of a cul-de-sac. Bisley was semi-rural; the house semi-detached.

Following Dad's trusted routine, I established a garden in which we grew vegetables and kept rabbits (that Dad helpfully provided) – as pets for the children rather than for the table. Finbarr and Kiera went to the local school, just around the corner. Rosie and I were young parents and still learning the trade as the children developed into thinking little people. We talked to them a lot and they both quickly learned good vocabularies, in advance of most of their peers. We were good friends together, Rosie, Finbarr, Kiera and I.

I was again working as a design engineer, on cryogenic air separation plants. I enjoyed working with this technology for the cryogenic gas processing plant and, usually, a set of pretty serious compressors. Understanding the equipment and matching instrumentation and controls to it was interesting. At this time, process instrumentation was primarily pneumatic; electronics were not as reliable and had no cost or performance advantage. We designed two pairs of plants for South Africa – one pair to be built in Newcastle, Natal and one pair for Vanderbijlpark in the Transvaal.

The plants were constructed under the supervision of our construction crew and the time came to commission them. Newcastle was running when I was asked to commission the instrumentation at Vanderbijlpark. I got on a British Airways Jumbo for the journey. Apartheid was practised in South Africa and most other African countries didn't allow flights over their territory to the Republic, so we flew round rather than over Africa.

It was a very unpleasant feeling to be sat in that cabin in the night sky, with the engines droning, thinking about my family getting further away hour by hour. This was January and I had left England in mid-winter. I landed in Johannesburg to bright, searing sunshine and temperatures in the high 30s. I picked up a hire car and drove to the plant site at Vanderbijlpark, arriving in the late afternoon.

I was greeted by our start-up manager, Jack Fuller and his first orders were, "Go down to Newcastle; we have a few instrumentation problems that need to be sorted and it will be a week or so before you can really start here."

He added, "There is a room reserved for you at the Holiday Inn; you should get there in time for a night's sleep. Newcastle is that way, about 200 miles but, it's a straight road; you can't go wrong."

Well, it was a straight road, across the high veldt of The Transvaal and The Orange Free State; a single tarmac strip, brown grass as far as I could see and the odd gum tree. Apart from an occasional dirt road, off to a farm I supposed, there were no landmarks. The road gently undulated, but there were no bends for most of the way. After a few hours I longed for a bend, or to see another vehicle. I had got used to climbing each slight rise of the road in the expectation that the crest would offer a different view – but it never did. It got dark and there were no lights anywhere. I started to consider the reliability of the Ford Cortina and began to debate with myself whether the natives would be friendly, or if there would be any way of getting help if I needed it. Were there wild animals in this part of Africa? I had not done any research before setting out. Indeed, I had not expected to have been setting out; at least not to have been striking out across the high veldt, alone, at night.

Nearing Newcastle I came to a bend at last – and some hills. I had reached the Drakensburg Mountains of north-west Natal.

137

It wasn't hard to find the hotel; there were few buildings of any size and, the next morning, it wasn't hard to find the plant. My first task was to buy some safari suits – the preferred kit for this climate – green or fawn shorts and battle dress-type top. I visited the bush clothes' shop, but was not sure what to buy. I thought I'd get some advice at the plant and shop around later. Shops like this one were always owned by an Asian. I hadn't experienced Asian trading practices before and the more I tried to exit the shop, the lower the price became. The "customer engagement" was so emphatic that I realised I would not be able to leave without buying something – or causing a diplomatic incident. I bought two safari suits and the price was good.

The first problems I was asked to fix were with the analysers that did not seem to have been commissioned properly. This wasn't a problem for me; I was quite familiar with the types installed here. My five years in the refinery had familiarised me with most types of process instruments and analysers. It did take time, however, to set up and do the calibrations. The analysers were installed outside with just rain hoods to protect from the monsoon-type rains that occurred every afternoon in summer. There was no need for winterisation in this location. I hadn't worked in shorts before, or in the South African sun. After a couple of hours, stood with my back to the sun, I went to move and found my legs didn't seem to bend; the skin was baked hard. Remarkably, the sunburn was not too painful and I soon got over it.

I spent about a week at Newcastle, then returned to Vanderbijlpark where I checked into the Killarney Hotel – a good Afrikaans name! This was a seedy establishment. I imagine it had been quite smart when it was first opened, probably 20 or 30 years earlier, but now displayed flaking paint and grubby décor. My room was basic but comfortable enough.

We were 5000 feet above sea level and, from my design work, I remembered that the atmospheric pressure was 0.86 bar absolute. This was not enough altitude to cause any discomfort.

The crew on site was quite small: a process manager, process engineer, a couple of start-up technicians, a machinery engineer, an electrician and, now, me. The plant consisted of two cold boxes[1] containing the cryogenic equipment, two expansion engines, two air compressors, two nitrogen compressors and two oxygen compressors. I had the schedule for commissioning the plant and my job was to keep ahead of the process team, making sure the instrumentation was ready in time for them to commission each part of the plant. A half-hour meeting each morning kept me updated, so I could adjust priorities when necessary.

I worked alone, checking each instrument and making sure every control loop[2] worked. I did a full functional check on every item of the eighty or so control loops and on all other instrumentation. I even checked that the controllers' algorithms correctly calculated the required outputs. The loop checking required me to be in the control room, at the transmitter and at the control valve at the same time. Some of these items were on the coldboxes, up to 100 feet high. To accomplish this I simply ran up and down the coldbox stairways – three times for each loop to check zero, mid-point and full scale operation.

---

[1] A coldbox is a steel clad, steel framed structure, 10 to 15 feet square and about 100 feet high, that supports the equipment which is packed with an insulating material such as Rockwool or expanded perlite and purged with dry nitrogen to provide a moisture-free environment for the equipment that operated at temperatures as low as minus 191 C.

[2] A control loop consists of a measuring device that transmits a signal to a controller, which calculates an output, which goes to a final control element such as a control valve, all to automatically maintain the controlled variable at the desired value.

It's a shame I wasn't rowing at this time; the altitude training would have helped my performance.

Most items were fine and I corrected any design, wiring and piping errors as I went. When I got to the compressors, I found the Hagan anti-surge controllers had been incorrectly specified and the wrong models were installed. The correct items would not have been much different and I could re-configure what I had with a few simple new parts. We were a long way from home and the quickest way to achieve this was to use the bench-fitting skills learned at the Apprentice Training Centre. Here, there was no Roger to scatter my tools and I accomplished the modifications in a couple of days.

As an only-child I had learned self-reliance and on the commissioning job I was effective. This job didn't need much team work. Engineering is often like that; in most situations we need self-reliant people who can get things done. Respect for others and a little tolerance is all that is needed. Teamwork can be very frustrating. Teamwork, which is always spoken of in a positive way, is when people rely on each other and need a social element in their working life. How is this positive for getting things done?

About 25% of people in the population are only-children, but when I reflect on the lads I served my apprenticeship with, I think we were more than 50%. Engineering, especially in the engineering trades, seems to attract us.

In those days Air Products Limited (APL) was a fairly autonomous subsidiary of the American parent company, but we did sometimes hear from the Americans. Americans seemed to be very keen on teamwork and they talked about it as though it was self-evident that teamwork was a good thing; a thing we should all aspire to. I came to appreciate a lot of American values. For example, they have a strong work ethic and a direct, unambiguous approach to business. Although they are not necessarily very efficient, they do have a great focus on getting results.

What is more difficult to accept is their unquestioning belief that all their values are the best and should be adopted by the whole world. Apart from any other considerations, this would be bad for social evolution and would restrict progress by dampening innovation on social issues; a global uniformity would be dangerous.

I worked every day and, as the plants were started up, occasionally nights as well. One night when I wasn't working I was woken by McKenzie's booming Scots voice, "You're naded ait the plant: we've gat a problem."

When I got there I found the plant had tripped; a distillation column level had got too high when its controller had been put into manual mode and the operator (McKenzie) wasn't watching. When the start-up manager, Jack, arrived in the morning, McKenzie asserted that the column needed an extra alarm to prevent recurrence. Jack advised McKenzie to watch the plant more closely in future. The right result, but this was just the beginning of a new attitude in engineering: the prima donna process engineer. Up to this time it had been understood that an engineer should be thoroughly trained, experienced and responsible and his work didn't need checking because he made sure he got it right. What we were seeing in McKenzie's attitude was a new, "I need to be cosseted and it isn't my fault if I make a mistake" attitude that I would see grow to epidemic proportions over the next 30 years, as training became briefer and individuals became more mobile in their jobs.

From time to time, another engineer would visit to apply his speciality and go home again. My three week assignment became three months. There was almost no social element in my life in Vanderbijlpark and I didn't have spare time to visit any game parks or see any wild animals. I did send postcards of elephants to the children and of bare-breasted African beauties to my dad.

I ate in the Killarney hotel every evening. For my entertainment, they had an endless tape machine. Unfortunately they only had one tape, so *The Legend of the Glass Mountain* came around every 45 minutes. Albert, the Zulu waiter, took good care of me. I gave him a tip of 5 Rand a week (my income would have been about £40 - 250 Rand - a week) and he seemed very happy with this. The menu was simple but the food was good and wholesome. Typically, there were three items of each; the starter, the main course and the dessert to choose from. Albert never took my order; he simply brought me three starters, three main courses and three desserts: good fuel for coldbox running. To break the routine, I decided to dress for dinner on Saturday evenings. I would have a shave, bathe and put on shirt, tie and jacket; and my black Jeeves would wait on me to the music of Mantovani and his orchestra. I usually had the restaurant to myself.

Living and working in The Transvaal, I was able to observe apartheid first hand. In Vanderbijlpark, the shops that blacks were allowed to use had two entrances marked "Europeans" and "Non-whites" and a counter running down the middle so the staff could serve both sides.

There were formal and informal protocols for the behaviour of the different races. In order of descending privilege, there were Europeans, Asians, Coloureds and Bantu (the black native people). When we had an American visitor, we told him he couldn't use any of the toilets because he wasn't European or brown or black.

A contractor supplying workers would have a "Boss Man" - always white, a "Boss Boy" - always black - and black labourers. Tradesmen were Afrikaners. "Afrikaner" was supposed to mean "all the people of Africa", but in practice it meant a white Boer descendent.

The British descendents called these people "Yarpies", a pejorative term intended to promote the British descendents to yet another level of privilege or, sometimes, "white wogs" to further emphasis the perceived inferiority.

Although a tradesman such as an electrician would be an Afrikaner, he would have a black "boy" to carry his tools and do most of the work. When I saw an Afrikaner beating his "boy" and asked him what he was doing, he told me that they had to be kept in their place and needed a beating from time to time.

On occasions, when not observed by the Boss Man, I would talk to the Bantu workers on the plant. They were well educated and most spoke at least three languages: English, Afrikaans and a Bantu language. One lunch hour I was sat with a group of Bantu workers, talking. There was suddenly alarm, sandwiches were thrown into the air and the men ran towards the plant where they were supposed to be working. The Boss Man was running towards them screaming and wielding a sjambok with which he flailed the slower members of the group. A sjambok is a leather whip about four feet long; it is about 1½ inches diameter at one end (the handle) and tapers to a fine tip. I imagine it is designed to inflict pain without doing damage that could affect the victim's ability to work.

Apartheid, established to maintain the superior position of three million whites in a country with twelve million blacks, did not create a pleasant atmosphere. The blacks, indeed, did seem to "know their place", but even if Apartheid worked as intended, the suppression of the human spirit and denial of the talents of the majority of the population was not a formula for the advancement of humanity.

Nelson Mandela was 12 years into his eventual 27 years in prison, but eventually apartheid, this failed social experiment, would be discontinued.

143

It was a very good feeling in the cabin of the Jumbo jet, heading for home. There was some satisfaction with the work I had done, but it was good to be leaving that unhappy country. After a small bottle of wine with an airline meal and a couple of glasses of whisky, I relaxed into semi-sleep, dreaming about my family that was getting closer hour by hour.

At Heathrow, Rosie and two pale, runny-nosed, English-winter-children were waiting to greet me. The welcome as Rosie threw her arms around me drew me instantly back from the unhappiness of The Transvaal to the comfort of my family and reminded me why I had been away. Finbarr had been primed to be pleased to see Daddy. Kiera was not at all sure who this suntanned person who embraced her mother was.

I settled back into the office routine, but it always took a week or so to adapt to the sedentary and claustrophobic conditions after a period of "freedom" on site. However, the work was interesting. I enjoyed doing the calculations. In those days we kept a calculation book that could be reviewed in case of questions or changes. The books were pages of log table calculations, dated and attributed to the project, the item tag number and the originator. Calculating machines were available, but these were unable to do square roots so were not suitable for engineering calculations until, one exciting day, a Wang electronic calculator, capable of extracting square roots, appeared. This sat proudly on its own desk and could be "booked" by an engineer.

I travelled to Germany for a meeting with an instrument manufacturing company. Now, all I knew about Germans was that they had bombed us and given my dad a hard time. Oh, also, one had married Tom's sister causing Dad to exclaim, "I don't know why I spent six years keeping the buggers out if she was just going to marry one."

144

Strangely, when I got there, I found they were courteous, hard working, and competent and they spoke my language: engineering. Also, they had families and, well, they were just like us. As I travelled around the world over the years I would find that the working man was the same everywhere, with aspirations only to take care of a family and have a job in which he felt valued.

I went to Japan where I found that, just like the Germans, here were people who just wanted to take care of their families and earn their living practising a satisfying profession. There were some cultural differences, but these were really quite superficial. I was working with a company in Yokohama, but for some reason I was billeted in a hotel in Tokyo. I became a Japanese commuter for the daily train journey. When I first arrived, everyone had slanty eyes and the same hair cut, but after a few days they metamorphosed into Europeans, with different noses, eyes, face shapes and some balding. I had noticed that a woman would always walk behind her husband as they boarded the train and, if there was only one seat, the man would take it.

One day I decided to try a culture blend. I watched a middle aged couple board the train on which there were no vacant seats and waited 'til the man had passed me. I then stood up, between the man and the seat and gestured to the woman to take my seat. She was flustered and very reluctant to sit. I re-emphasised my gesture and she sat down, looking very unhappy. The husband now turned round to see his wife sitting. He became upset, angry and paced up and down the aisle muttering like a samurai warrior. I had the distinct impression that, if he had been carrying his katana, he would have taken my head off. I now realised this had been irresponsible and I had caused a lot of distress.

I retreated, a little, as the man worked out how to honourably resolve the situation. He didn't want to offend me, but he couldn't bear the ignominy of his wife seated while he stood. He sat on her and we completed our journey in cautious silence.

The atmosphere in the engineering office in Yokohama was formal. Grey suited businessmen were being introduced in the foyer and greeting each other with careful attention to protocol – the most junior bowing the deepest. In meetings the more junior staff continually made a show of deferring to the more senior and, if asked a question by a superior, an engineer would exclaim with an enthusiastic "Hei," to leave no doubt that he was giving his full attention.

The purpose of my visit was to check that the interfaces between my company's designs and those of the Japanese were fully compatible. We found significant differences so, on the first evening, I worked in my hotel room and modified my circuits. I re-drew the details and went prepared for the meeting the following day. I had worked hard. I could immediately see the Japanese were impressed. That is, the senior engineer was impressed with my work, but disappointed that his man had done less. The discomfort was palpable, but the meeting went well enough.

That evening I followed the same routine and, the following morning, the Japanese response matched what I had done. The next day we, on both sides, seemed to have more to do and I was now working until 1 am. This became the pattern until the Saturday. This was not a normal working day and the office was much more informal, to the extent that I seemed to be able to wander around without a chaperone.

I went looking for my counterpart and was directed to his office. He didn't seem very pleased to receive me there and I could see that he had half a dozen men working on the designs. This was why my working hours had escalated; Mr. Osaki had reinforcements.

I spent only a couple of weeks in Japan, but I learned some of their social protocols and enjoyed working with them. They were polite and industrious and they spoke my language: engineering.

Chapter 14

Allentown, Pa

Business was still not booming in the UK and the company asked me to take an assignment at head office in Allentown, Pennsylvania. This is the town chosen in the musical *42nd Street* as stereotypical small-town America. I was reluctant; we hadn't been back in the UK for long and I didn't like Americans who were over confident and loud – just like public school English people. The trouble with Americans, I supposed, was that their country would be full of them. After some prevarication and negotiating a reasonable remuneration, I accepted and we went as a family to the USA. We arrived for Thanksgiving weekend – not the best time to arrive when the natives were all bound up in this peculiarly American festival, but we were not yet tuned into the culture and it hadn't occurred to us that the third Thursday in November was a holiday.

Pennsylvania was getting cold, very cold and 1974/75 would be a long, cold winter. The natives all but hibernated, just rushing from heated homes to heated automobiles to heated offices. However, is wasn't long before we realised that all the brash, loud Americans were in England and those left at home were well mannered, thoughtful and hard working – just like Germans and Japanese – and some English people.

We spent our first two weeks in the George Washington Hotel on Rt. 22 and 7th Street. Well, the children spent the first two weeks in the swimming pool of the George Washington Hotel, with Rosie as lifeguard while I started work at head office – in Trexlertown (T-town) – just down Rt. 222.

T-town was the corporate headquarters of Air Products and Chemicals Inc. (APCI). It was, and still is, a growing campus style development. At that time it was set in a

Pennsylvania Dutch farming area and was surrounded by thousands of acres of sweetcorn.

We rented a modern apartment on 15th Street. This was beautifully equipped with 1½ baths (I could only find one, but there was a shower as well), dishwasher, giant fridge and lots of space. It was unfurnished but it was easy to buy furniture in Allentown.

Rosie had taken a liking to the mock oil lamps that were popular and we bought one: a nice table lamp, but it only a day or two before our active 4-year-old smashed it. It was a bad idea anyway and we replaced it with a hanging Tiffany style lamp, which was pretty expensive, but they were only dollars. We got it back to the apartment and started to unwrap it. While we were offering up the main fitting to decide the best location, the sight of an "empty" box full of tissue paper proved too tempting for the boy with wrecking skills. He was in mid-air on a trajectory for the carefully wrapped glass parts in the box when we realised our second error. It was too late.

Our apartment was in a complex of about a hundred 2 and 3-bedroomed residences with a swimming pool, tennis and basketball courts. The residents' association needed a chairman and they elected me; the Americans said I would understand meeting protocol because I was English, so I should have the job. Actually, we learned that the English accent and vocabulary endowed us with a perceived intelligence. Although there are exceptions, many Americans manage only a limited vocabulary and a mangled version of English. We would hear, "I just love your accent," probably once a day.

Allentown, which is located in the Lehigh Valley, was not a place visited by tourists. It had been a self-contained farming area, populated by the descendants of German farmers that had become known as the Pennsylvania Dutch (Dutch was a corruption of Deutsch). Their neighbours to the south-west in the adjacent Lancaster County, the religious groups Amish and Mennonites, kept to themselves. To the north are the lightly populated Poconos, the local part of the Appalachian Mountains, which run from Maine to Georgia. To the south-east is Bethlehem, which was a Moravian settlement in the 18th century, but by 1850 had become one of America's most important steel towns and grew wealthy on the demand for its products stimulated by the two world wars. The steel industry was still important in 1975, but would decline until its shutdown in 1995 when steel production had moved to the Orient.

With its neighbouring urban areas, Allentown was middle class America and, by 1975, there were few new incomers except the graduates who came to work in the four big companies: Bethlehem Steel, Kraft, Mack Trucks and APCI. At the time these companies offered secure employment. The Brits, just a handful, who came to APCI were a novelty. We were not seen as threat by the confident people of the Lehigh Valley and these generous, friendly, honest and hard working people made us welcome. At first the compliments on everything from our accent to our children seemed disingenuous, but we soon learned that they were sincere: they were just less reserved than us.

I think Finbarr had a very good time when he started school: his accent, manners and, initially, the way we dressed him in shirt and tie set him apart and he was given celebrity status.

My assignment was with the Instrument Design department under the management of Benny Andrews and his two lieutenants, Earl Conroy and Ray Hengstler. I have worked with Americans all my life and, as I have said, they generally have a strong work ethic. The exception proves the rule and, here, I had found the exception. The reason they wanted me, I soon realised, was to do the work while the gentlemen in charge directed their attention to the more social aspects of business – lunches, Instrument Society of

151

America business (dinners) and frequent breaks to visit the Eagle Hotel to play shuffleboard. I didn't mind this at all and very much enjoyed working with colleagues across the company and interacting with vendors.

All manufacturers and suppliers of a corporation like APCI sold through agents. An agent, who was usually based in Philadelphia, 50 miles away down the turnpike, could make a good living if he kept his customer happy and maintained a steady stream of orders. His primary mechanisms for achieving this were twofold.

First, he would be responsive to his customer and drop everything to drive up to T-town and sit down at "his desk" and specify the equipment – control valves, transmitters or whatever – then take the order back to his office for processing. If he got anything wrong it was his responsibility to sort it out without embarrassing Benny or his men.

In the UK, I had been used to doing this work, then supervising the vendors to make sure they got it right and it had been my responsibility to sort out any problems. We just didn't have vendors with agents to trust to follow the American system. The Philadelphia agent generally drove a Cadillac and he knew his next new Cadillac depended on keeping Benny happy.

His other role was to buy lunch. In my ignorance I made a serious mistake that threatened my stay in the US when I had a meeting with a vendor who duly offered to take me to lunch. I accepted, but committed, the unforgivable sin of not checking that Benny had lunch that day. Benny did not and couldn't remember when he had last bought this own lunch. There was no "special relationship" between The USA and Britain that afternoon.

The professional class in Allentown were comfortable; they enjoyed a good income and lived in spacious homes with good services. Middle aged men, who accounted for most of the office population, tended to be a little

152

overweight and with that flaccid skin that hasn't seen a lot of sun or air. They did mention golf a lot, but I wondered if they actually played the game.

There was not a lot of excitement and almost no culture: I suppose people travelled the 50 miles to Philadelphia or the 86 miles to New York if they needed that. In their work they were competent, conscientious and self-assured. They were polite and pleasant. I loved the blending of cultures: they were all unmistakably American, but at the same time they were Italian, Irish, Greek or British – in the way that chop-suey served in the USA or Europe is Chinese; not fully authentic, but romanticised versions of the originals.

A man seemed to take his cue from his name and would build on it what he took to be the appropriate behaviour. When two or more with names from the same "old country" got together, they would accentuate their acting and learn catchy expressions from one another. Some weren't sure where they came from, but often had interesting names, such as the impressively named King Kadoo who was, of course, a Project Manager.

I found it refreshing to live and work in the USA, which is free from the British class system. America has its own systems of privilege, but not our pervasive, entrenched system in which an individual is instantly assessed and assigned his or her place. In Britain we are so used to it that we don't notice it, but looking back from the openness of American society, it was clear to see. America has its "preppies" – those who went to the more expensive schools and Ivy League universities. They expect to do better in their careers, but socially their "superiority" is managed so as not to be too offensive. In Britain, the 7% who attend public schools expect to - and do - populate what they like to call "the professions", but it is socially where they are particularly divisive – in the anachronistic way they maintain their "superior" distance by speech and fussy behaviour.

We needed a car. Actually we needed a car just to cross the road; there were very few sidewalks and very little provision for pedestrians. To appreciate the American experience I purchased a '68 Oldsmobile Delta 88 Coupe. The engine was 455 cubic-inches – I make that 6½ litres – and the bonnet was nearly 7 feet square. It cruised beautifully at the national speed limit of 55 mph and coped well with the 15 mph neighbourhood limit.

Rosie was distressed one day when I got home from the office. The Olds had a dent. She had been in the car park of the YMCA, the only place in Allentown with a swimming pool, and a man had reversed into our car. She said he had been fairly uncompromising, but she had managed to get his details and phone number. I phoned him.

"Is that Mr. Isaacs?"

"Speaking."

"I think you had a small accident today in the car park at the Y?"

"Yes."

"It was my car. My wife was driving. I expect you would like to pay for the damage."

"No."

"But I think it was your fault and my car is damaged."

"It may have been my fault but it was on private land and there is nothing you can do."

"Forgive me for saying this, but that is not a very Christian attitude."

"I'm a Jew," he said as he put the phone down. I thought he sounded smug.

There it is again: that Jewish thing. But it's all part of the richness of diversity. And he had put me in my place. It was clumsy of me to assume that everyone would aspire to being a Christian.

Americans are wonderfully practical. There are "Snow Routes" clearly marked and, if you drive on one of these in snow and, if your car is not fitted with snow tyres and, if you get stuck, there is a fine. If you are lucky enough to have a sidewalk outside your house, it is your responsibility to keep it clear. If you don't and someone is injured, you get fined – or sued. We had a lot of snow that winter. This gave us picturesque views and lots of fun for the children (now called kids) in their K-Mart snow suits and snow shoes, on their K-Mart toboggans. Allentown has pleasant parks with grassy slopes, just right for junior snow activities. One day in April, the season changed from winter to summer; no spring. Later in the summer, we decided on a trip to the beach. The Jersey coast seemed to be the closest but was still a long drive. When we got there we found a nice enough beach, although a bit commercialised. We took up a spot on the sand and broke out the picnic. In minutes, a uniformed quasi-military type informed us we were not allowed food on the beach. There was a nice little, seaweed covered breakwater and we thought the children might use the ham sandwiches to catch crabs.

Another visit from the Gestapo; apparently you were not allowed to walk on the seaweed in case you slipped and sued the municipality. Swimming; we'll go swimming we thought and jumped into the sea. A lifeguard appeared and informed us we were swimming in the "surfing area". This was not allowed even though there were no surfers. We moved a 100 yards up the beach to the "swimming area", which was crowded. I'll just swim out beyond the masses and float for a while I thought; I needed to relax. Another lifeguard and this one was angry that he had to come out to tell me I was too far out (you don't hear the whistle with your ears under water). It was time to begin the long drive home anyway.

One of my pleasant, slightly overweight, flaccid- skinned colleagues decided to get some fresh air and he organised a canoe trip down the Delaware River. About a dozen families joined the expedition in hired Indian style canoes made of "aluminum". We were going downstream, so it was quite easy paddling. After a couple of hours we noticed a sign: "Grade 6 Rapids". We wondered what that meant. Around the bend we found out that a grade-6 rapid had fast water and lots of rocks. The first crew to test their skills hit a rock and their canoe folded around it, trapping one canoeist by her legs. She was extracted safely and we continued through the noisy, turbulent waves. Rosie, sat in the front, decided to scream. The children, sat in the middle, decided to scream. I sat at the rear skilfully and coolly steering first one side, then the other to slalom round the rocks; a very satisfying trip.

The work continued to be interesting and, although I think I worked as hard as anyone and harder than some, it seemed altogether an easier pace than in the UK. The company had a close association with the local university, Lehigh, and a course in cryogenic engineering was offered, with the lecturer coming to the company once a week.

I enrolled and completed the course and improved my understanding of cryogenic process technology. I suppose I have one tenth of a Master's Degree from Lehigh; the cryogenic module was worth 3 points and 30 were needed for the degree.

The annual leave allowance in the US was only two weeks a year compared with the four weeks at home, but we were able to use this to make two trips to see a bit of North America.

The first, in June, was to Canada. We drove north through New York State to Niagara where we crossed into Canada. The falls were spectacular – one and a half million gallons a second of water flows over the two parts of the falls: The Bridal Veil and The Horseshoe. When I got home I found I had taken 8 rolls of film of the same scene. It is the sheer grandeur of such places that draws people to them. At Niagara it is the swirling plumes of mist and the ceaseless thunder of the water; an immense natural energy in evidence. Travel in the US and Canada was easy with good roads and plenty of comfortable motels, always with vacancies. The roadside diners serve excellent meals and the breakfasts are particularly enjoyable with lashings of fresh bacon, eggs, grits, pancakes – all piled on one plate – and non-stop coffee.

We made our way, crossing the Napanee River and onto Toronto where we spent a pleasant sojourn touring the city and visiting the park, which is on an offshore island. We continued north and east to circumnavigate Lake Ontario, returning along the St. Lawrence River. At one stopping point we saw a turtle crossing the road and I thought I would make a contribution to conservation by helping it to safety. I discovered that a turtle is not at all like a tortoise – it can move very fast and this one was a "snapper" with a beak which, I was later advised, could chomp off a finger. Luckily I had picked this one up by the sides of the shell and I was able to keep my fingers.

We enjoyed the wildlife we saw in North America, in parks, forest and by the roadside, including prairie dogs, chipmunks, squirrels, skunks, fireflies, praying mantises and many unfamiliar brightly coloured birds.

Later in the summer we made a tour to North Carolina, driving along the Blue Ridge Mountains through Tennessee. There was much to entertain us. In addition to the scenery, there were roadside attractions like the Tweetsie Railroad where a western gunfight was re-enacted and mice worked in a cheese mine. This was a minor theme park in America, but was more delightful and more frivolous than anything to be found in Britain at that time.

Enthusiasm was growing for the celebration of the "Bicentennial" of the USA. I did not get the impression that many Americans knew much about their history, but they knew this was a good thing and they lived in the land of the free. Independence was declared in 1776, but the 200th

anniversary was a good excuse to stretch the commercialisation of the event over two years and they started in 1975. This must have been a boost for the still fledgling Chinese economy; America needed lots of flags and commemorative tat that could best be made cheaply in China and the Orient.

America moves smoothly from one festival to another – Halloween to Thanksgiving to Christmas to St. Patrick's Day, to Easter, with Mother's Day, Father's Day, Veteran's day, Happy Hanukkah and many others to fill any perceived gaps. The bi-centennial was laid comfortably on top of all this and enjoyed by all, especially the retailers.

There was work involved in the assignment to Allentown, but overall it felt like a holiday; it changed my perception of Americans and is an experience Rosie and I cherish.

Most English assignees to Allentown went for one or two years and stayed five or ten. We certainly enjoyed our time there, but to stay longer would have been to settle down and move to accommodation with a garden. Apartment living is fine as a temporary convenience, but family life needs a bit more. On balance we decided to head home.

It had been a good experience and getting to know many of my American colleagues helped me in communication and trust over the next 30 years and made my occasional business visits to head office enjoyable.

We could now enjoy a reasonably comfortable standard of living on my salary. Boosted a little financially by our American assignment, we had made enough money to buy a new car and some furniture. The car, an estate, was the much maligned Austin Allegro, but it served us very well. The furniture was the fashionable G-Plan. Up to this point I had experienced only second-hand purchases and we were now blending into middle class England – not that this had been an ambition; it just happened.

We were fortunate not to be as badly affected as many others by the poor state of the economy. I settled into family and business life in the UK and gradually worked my way up the organisation. At work, the technology I was working with had been gradually refined, but had not fundamentally changed for 30 years. However, each time I felt my interest was waning, there was a promotion that added scope to my job.

We got Finbarr settled into the village school and Rosie and Kiera settled into the community – such as it was. Bisley was something of a dormitory village with a transient community of commuters. I worked, Rosie took care of things at home, we visited family and they visited us. For our holidays we went to the West Country.

Chapter 15

Settling Down

1976 was my dad's 65th year. Although he had always kept fit, he had found the shift work hard in the later years and it was with some relief that he was thinking about his retirement, which would be on his birthday on 12 December.

He retired and drew his pension from 8 January. He seemed to be well, perhaps a bit overweight, and he was still robust with an imposing stature. When I counselled him to work on his waistline he would retort, "I came into this world hungry; I'm not going out hungry!"

It had been a long hard road, but he had paid for his house and had savings to ensure Mum's security. He said he couldn't understand why he was being paid and not going to work. Although I think you would say he was fully paid up; having worked since the age of fourteen, served for the full duration of the war, never drawn state benefit and had rarely, if ever, taken a day's paid sick-leave. He was not comfortable with the concept of receiving an income, modest as it was, without working. Otherwise, he was content in those weeks, working in his garden; that is, until early March when he suffered a stroke while working on his strawberry bed. He felt sick, came indoors and lay down on the bed. When he lost consciousness, Mum had called the ambulance and he was taken to Southampton General. By the time I had driven down to be with them at the hospital, Mum had been advised, "There is nothing you can do. Go home and we'll call you if there is any change."

He was in a ward with just a curtain around his bed. I sat with him for a while. I asked tentatively if he could hear me. No response at all.

I promised I would look after Mum, but inhibited by my awareness of the occupants of the adjacent beds, I didn't try very hard to get a response. Probably none could have come, but I should have tried harder. I took Mum home.

We didn't talk; Mum hoping that "any change" could mean improvement and me not daring to think about it without more data. Dad had overcome every obstacle placed before him in his life: he had extracted himself from having to crawl under synagogue floors, had shrugged off the displeasure of the world heavyweight boxing-cum-wrestling champion, coped with a failed marriage, fought off the Nazi threat, worked through his personal economic depression after the war and survived an accident that could have killed or blinded him. We had always imagined he was indestructible and it was obvious that he would live forever, or at least to a great age. We now suspended logic and dared to hope this would be just another blip.

After a night of little sleep for me and, I'm sure, of no sleep for Mum, we got up and continued without conversation. Mrs Lovell came round from next door to say that there was a telephone call for Mum. My parents were still too "careful" - or trained not to by years of forced frugality – to have a phone.

"He's dying," she sobbed when she returned. "They said we should come at once."

I drove: along the Marchwood bypass, overtaking where I shouldn't have, racing over Totton Causeway, down Tebourba Way; fifteen miles to the hospital. We arrived at the ward to the news that we were too late.

Death came that day, cut down my father and took him away. Was this right? Had there been a proper assessment – all those years of work, taxes all paid, clean shaven, shoes shone, always on time, country served, family taken care of? And it was too soon. We weren't ready.

Mum was numb, shocked, devastated and it was so heart rending to hear her cry "My lovely Georgie."

I felt ashamed that I had not talked to Dad in his coma, shouted at him, done everything to communicate with him – just in case he could hear those moments at his bedside. This was a surprising way for Dad to go. He had been happily adjusting to his retirement and seemed fit; in fact, had been declared fit. Mum had made sure he saw the GP for a check-up at regular intervals. After his death, I went to see the GP, seeking some understanding of the inconceivable.

"Your father hasn't been to see me for more than 10 years," I was informed.

Dad had "confused" the Hampshire Yeoman's public bar with the doctor's surgery all those years and happily informed Mum after each visit, "I'm fine."

Mum never got over his death, but continued to be self-sufficient and she never put any demands on me, but I am not sure I did as much as I could have for her. I am sure she enjoyed seeing such success as I achieved in life and it may have been sufficient that I led the life they had worked to make possible for me. I too had worked hard and taken my opportunities. My challenges had been less and I never did fight for the Queen. There is much for my generation to be grateful for: a fair liberal democracy and a chance to live in peace and provide a family with education and opportunity.

I have a great deal to thank my father for; he provided for me, guided me and gave me a great example to follow. Whenever I got a daft idea about not completing my apprenticeship or working contract for a short-term increase in income, he gently counselled me and kept me on the straight and narrow and emphasised the value of a secure job.

I spent a little time with Mum, then returned to my family. This was a busy time in my life and there was much to distract me from my grief, but Mum would have to come to terms with it and find a new life for herself.

She came to stay with us to enjoy her grandchildren from time to time and I taught her to drive. She had never considered a need to do this and driving had always been considered a man's job. She surprised herself by adapting to this new skill with enthusiasm and the determination that had got her through life to this point now enabled her to become independently mobile.

I am pleased that, in many ways, I am like my dad; there is the family resemblance, but also, I think I have inherited some of his thought processes. I cannot guess whether this is genetic or mimetic – just absorbed through nurture. When I am working with my hands, I still see my dad's hands doing the work. I suppose I spent a lot of time watching him and scrutinising the detail as we did projects together around the garden, making chicken houses and fences; also fishing – tying line and baiting hooks.

1977 was the Queen's Silver Jubilee year. I am not a royalist having, I suppose, been born with a distain for privilege and, as I had got closer to it, became convinced that, indeed, it had become a bar to further social evolution. I was not born with any sort of spoon in my mouth, certainly not a silver one, but thanks to the National Health Service, I did have a cod liver oil spoon in my mouth for much of my childhood.

The royal family is, at the same time, both the pinnacle and the foundation of privilege. It will be difficult or impossible for society to progress towards the fair, secure and prosperous society we must surely aspire to as long as we keep them. On the positive side, the system of privilege that drove the British Empire had led the world to industrialisation, technology and democracy and there is much to be valued and preserved. I do advocate change, but history has taught that revolution always retards progress.

With an ageing monarch and an unadmirable string of heirs, we may be approaching the time to dissolve the

164

monarchy and build on the democracy we have achieved: evolution, not revolution.

There was to be a jubilee celebration in the village, the centre piece of which would be a jubilee themed fancy dress competition and procession. It seemed, even for a republican, like a good idea for neighbours to come together in a spirit of community and we made a "coronation coach" out of old boxes, wallpaper and pram wheels. Kiera, with cardboard crown, was the queen and Finbarr on his bike decorated with red, white and blue crepe paper was the footman and horses. There was a good turnout and I think we all enjoyed the day.

I was commuting to the office in New Malden, sometimes cycling to Brookwood station for the train, or, to save money, sharing a tedious, traffic choked drive. I bought an old AJS 350 cc "Jampot" and enjoyed riding that to work. After living expenses, there was very little spare money. I had kept some of my old riding gear, but I had to wear Wellington boots, as new leather riding boots seemed like an unnecessary investment. One day I forgot to carry shoes to work and had to wear the wellies all day. I pulled my trousers over the boots and tried to be as inconspicuous as possible. Unfortunately, that was the day I was called to a senior level meeting on the fifteenth floor; directors lived there and never visited the floors where ordinary mortals worked.

Bewellingtoned, I strode confidently into the meeting and declared that I must be in the shit if I was invited to a top floor meeting and had worn the wellies as a precaution. I suppose this just reminded the senior people why they didn't visit the engineering offices. It was, also, probably why the loos on the top floor had Yale locks with keys held only by those who preferred not to pee alongside someone in rubber boots.

165

Rosie and I never discussed family planning, although we had used contraception from the time we left Ireland. We had two lovely children, a boy and a girl, but it seemed like the right time to discontinue the use of the pill in late 1977. We were not completely sure that it would be safe to use for the long term.

It was good for society to have a controlled birth rate: from the government's perspective it seemed healthier if people had small families that they could look after effectively and, from the individual's perspective, a higher, or at least materialistically standard of living could be sustained. For these reasons the pill had become firmly accepted and widely used.

It had been more than 15 years since the thalidomide disaster, but it would be another 35 before there was a government apology for the errors. It was a Labour Government that would apologise for mistakes of Harold Macmillan's Conservative government. From 1959 thalidomide had been in use on NHS advice that it was safe, despite reports from around the world in the late 50s of abnormalities in babies whose mothers had previously taken it. Enoch Powell, who was Minister of Health from 1960 to 1963, had supported its use and declined government support for the victims after thalidomide was withdrawn in 1961. This left legal action as the only recourse of the affected families and Powell undermined that by stating that thalidomide had been properly tested. It was eventually proven that this was not the case and Distillers Pharmaceuticals paid some compensation.

This disgrace was twofold. Firstly, available data that would have urged caution was not used properly; then responsibility was evaded by the government. I suppose the apology was recognition that this quality of decision making and leadership was not what people should expect from their government.

Now, in the mid-70s, we were experiencing a controversy over the use of whooping cough vaccine that was blamed for brain damage in some children. From a societal risk point of view, the vaccine was, perhaps, a good thing as demonstrated by the marked increase of the disease as parents declined its use. For the individual family, however, it was clear to me that the small risk of whooping cough itself was preferable to the risk of brain damage, even though this was very small. Although whooping cough is unpleasant and distressing, it is rarely fatal, nor does it have long term ill effects. We were a robust family and I reasoned that our children would cope with the disease if it happened.

The weakness in the government's position was that they steadfastly refused to consider compensation for those who had apparently suffered brain damage from the vaccine. If I was to have my children vaccinated for the benefit of society, then society should accept responsibility for the few children who were damaged. We had had Finbarr and Kiera vaccinated against whooping cough before the risk had been established, but we would not do so with any further children.

We used mechanical contraceptive methods, but not very conscientiously and, not surprisingly, Rosie became pregnant again. When baby Katherine (Katie) was born in August 1978, Finbarr and Kiera were seven and six respectively.

This was our first baby in England. Rosie had a straightforward pregnancy, as with the first two. On the 7 August the contractions started at a convenient time in the morning. It was a Monday. I came home from work and took Rosie to St. Peter's hospital for the delivery, stopping only briefly when she threatened to give birth in the car.

There were no nuns at St. Peter's and I was able to be present at the birth. This was a great experience for me and Rosie said she liked the support of having me there, but I suppose the birth of the first child will always be the one to have the most impact. Rosie was good at having babies and, apart from a bit of groaning, it all seemed straightforward. However, she would stay in hospital for the four days allowed under the NHS, to have as much rest as possible.

The house in Bisley was the second we had bought from an enthusiastic, but incompetent do-it-yourselfer. We had worked on putting the kitchen right and accomplished that, but the main bedroom was a disastrous "fitted" design-as-you go creation of almost endless lengths of timber placed chaotically so as not to support the hardboard covering that bowed and sagged. In another 20 years it could have been exhibited in the Tate Modern, where art lovers who liked a statement that commented on the mundane would swoon as its primrose yellow, gloss painted contours reflected the light. It would probably be titled, "Monument to DIY in the 20th Century".

I suppose I did insufficient planning, but I was sure Rosie would be delighted if she came home to a new bedroom. I took time off work to look after the children and Rosie and Katie when they would come home. Rosie would be in St. Peter's Hospital for four days, just time I thought to work a minor miracle in the bedroom department.

As soon as Katie was born, I collected the older children from the friend we had lent them to for the day, parked them in front of the telly and set about stripping out the botched wardrobes and cupboards. For speed I threw the timber out of the window onto the front lawn. I ripped up the carpet and despatched that in the same way and I parked the bed on the landing. The walls and ceiling were now a mess of missing plaster and different paint finishes.

I filled the holes, rubbed down the door, door frame and skirting and repainted the lot.

Visiting times came round very quickly. I would wash the parts of the children that showed, pull a couple of sweet peas from the garden and visit mother and baby with Finbarr and Kiera coached into telling how well Daddy was looking after them ("Don't mention the junk food, late nights in front of the telly and lack of personal hygiene.") I had purchased a sliding wall wardrobe kit; I fitted that. New carpet was delivered; I fitted that. Also a new light fitting and the work was complete; just the mess to dispose of.

Rosie, on her third baby, had not been thrilled with the meagre sweet pea offering while other, first time, mums in the same ward couldn't be seen for the lavish floral arrangements that doting husbands had lovingly provided. The practice of banning flowers from hospitals came too late for me. The fourth day came and we brought Rosie and Katie home. When she saw the bedroom, she forgave me for the weaknesses of my flower provision.

The country was still sick with the British Disease. Harold Wilson had been elected on a manifesto promising a "social contract" and there had been some respite after the extreme lows of Ted Heath's government. However, Wilson was forced out by sinister forces and replaced by caretaker, Jim Callaghan. Some union leaders, now liking the power they had acquired, thought the social order could be changed.

Like all human institutions – religions, companies, public services – unions were established for honest reasons with good intentions, but their leaders forgot these and started to serve only their own interests and ambitions. 1978: enter Red Robbo, the union leader who thought he could use his platform as a British Leyland union leader to further his political ideals.

It turned out that the British Leyland workers were not entitled to jobs after all and he had done enough damage to cause the company to fold.

My dad would have been sad to see the corruption of power in trade union leadership that led to this ridiculous situation. Trade Unions were a major force in moving social progress, improving working conditions, wages and education; it was counter to social progress that they should be instrumental in the destruction of the means of production.

The unions are no better than the free market capitalists who they oppose if they do not act responsibly. Conversely, they are no worse; indeed they can never be quite as bad. It is the responsibility of the owners of capital and their appointed managers to create and maintain environments in which people can work effectively. This is what they are paid for and they must bear the accountability when there is conflict.

From early in the 20th century there had been militancy in the labour movement and, in these early days, this had been necessary to break, or at least crack, the mould (both meanings of *mould* can apply here) of exploitative employment practices. And it was logical that the same people who fought for workers' rights would support the establishment Labour Party and be involved in running it. However, ongoing direct involvement with the Party should have ceased at some point. We need unions as a strong, coherent voice of the workers to cooperate with government and employers' organisations and manage progress towards a society with fair and efficient industries.

It is undemocratic – now that we have a democracy – for union leaders to use the collective power of their members to pursue political agendas. We really need this to be sorted out: the Labour Party is probably our best bet for social progress.

The Conservative Party has a role in preserving the best from our past, but its very name – *Conservative* – signals resistance to change and their underlying priority is to preserve privilege. The Liberals (sorry, Liberal Democrats) have been so far from government for a hundred years that they have become indelibly prone to the impractical ideas and contradictions, safe in the knowledge that they will never have to do anything. It is unfortunate that those who formed the SDP (Social Democratic Party) - and eventually merged with the Liberals - mistimed their move, in 1991, to realign British politics. Tony Blair made a good start to his premiership and partially modernised the Labour Party at the very end of the century, but there is still plenty of room – and need – for progress.

We were not sure how big our family would become, but even if it remained at three children we did feel that we would need more space and we started to look for a suitable house that could be our long-term home. We could afford to increase our mortgage by around £10,000. This set our target property price at £40,000, which could get us a four-bedroomed house with a small garden, or something smaller with a bit more land. We chose the land and found a three-bedroomed, detached house with the space to enlarge at Fox Corner.

The house was only 25-years-old, but was in a poor state. However, we were excited by the potential and had plenty of energy. We imagined it would take us a couple of years to knock it into shape. In the first year we did make the house habitable, but it would take us another 20 years to get it to where we wanted it. With interest rates at 15%, we had to pace further investment; we also needed to do much of the work ourselves - and there would be distractions.

This was a busy time in our lives with a lot to think about. One thing we did not think enough about was family planning and Rosie's next pregnancy was a surprise. As with Katie, this eventually, at the end of June, involved a trip to St. Peter's on a Monday. When her contractions started and had progressed to come in close intervals, I took Rosie to the maternity ward, having left Katie with our friend and neighbour, Elaine Kelly, who would also collect the others from school. When I was expelled, I wondered if the nurse on guard duty had trained in Cork. Each hour I approached the desk to enquire whether I could join my wife, each time to be asked to wait. I now had a bit of experience of Rosie's childbirth style and I felt sure that, after a couple of hours, it was now time. Anyway, I knew my wife wished to have me with her. I insisted on being allowed in and, this time, successfully breached the defences of the guard. I had been at Rosie's side only a few minutes when Edward greeted the world.

After moving to Fox Corner, we had become friendly with Elaine and her husband David. They had two children, each a year younger than Finbarr and Kiera and we all got along well. The Kellys were members of the United Reformed Church (URC), which was a few hundred yards from our home. I didn't know what the URC was, but I had inherited a suspicion of churches and had assumed the URC was an obscure sect. However, Elaine and David were perfectly normal. When they invited us to take the children to Sunday school we accepted, thinking that any help bringing up our children would be appreciated. The people we met at the church were pleasant company and we started to enjoy going along. Of course, religion was all superstitious nonsense and I, with my scientific view of life, was above all the churchy stuff.

I listened with this detachment for quite some time, but gradually came to realise that my scientific knowledge did not give me any more answers and no more understanding of life or human nature. One of the most interesting members of the URC was a man who had worked all his life as a gardener. From his conversation and conduct it was apparent that he had spent his solitary hours with the spade in quiet contemplation and had achieved a good balance in life.

For some time I had been nurturing the idea of studying for an engineering degree. I was no longer making the long business trips to commission new plants and this seemed to be the best opportunity I would get. Although a degree wasn't strictly necessary for my career with APL, it could only increase my potential to progress. Also, I needed to prove to myself that I really was good enough.

I negotiated a 20% reduction in pay and a day off a week and started a four year part-time degree course in the September. In the event, my boss was supportive and sponsored me to do the course with no reduction in salary, but reduced annual pay rises. With inflation running at around 15%, this was not a lot different to taking a cut, but the support was appreciated.

The course, in mechanical engineering, was at the South Bank Polytechnic and it turned out to be well directed and well run. I had an HNC and this allowed me to start the degree programme without the need to complete a bridging course. Also, I had done work on my own to refresh the academic part of my brain that had been resting for more than ten years. The first year was very challenging and there was a high drop-out rate, but with Rosie's support and encouragement I persevered and got through. Some of the lecturers were a little pedestrian, but a couple were exceptional and I drew great encouragement from the stimulation of their lectures.

174

Chapter 16

I've got the Foreman's Job at Last

The Instrument Design Section, part of the Design Engineering Department, had half a dozen engineers and about the same number of draughtsmen – usually known as "Designers". I enjoyed my work as a design engineer and don't think I was ready to move into management, but when the position of Section Head – the first rung on the management ladder – became vacant, I applied. Although the extra money would be useful, I was more motivated by the satisfaction of being able to do what I considered to be a worthwhile and intellectually rewarding job and, anyway, I had only just embarked on the degree course. However, I did not wish to work for the other senior engineer in the section whom I considered to be rather staid and I feared he might limit my ability to be innovative.

I was a little surprised to be successful and I moved into the office in January 1981. All other members of the team worked in an open plan area, but "the boss" had a small office. The office facilities' team put my name on the door in plug-in plastic letters (not too permanent and easily revised). They were revised; the next morning the name on my office door was not "P G Morley" but "Worpy leg". I was pleased that my new subordinates had the humour to tinker in this way.

Rosie and I have only hazy memories of this period; this is probably because we were now running on autopilot with survival as the only objective.

I received no training in management and just had to watch the other managers and work it out. Initially I knew no better than to be simply a senior engineer. I would assign work to members of the team and do the most challenging calculations and configurations myself.

I had ideas on improving quality and efficiency, but no idea how to engage my workforce. I just assumed good ideas would be self-evident and, therefore, automatically accepted. Well, of course, this did not happen and, especially from the more senior engineers, there was resistance to change.

We had formal Engineering Standards, but very few procedures. I would judge what work to check and how carefully to check it. The work of senior engineers or designers would receive only cursory review, except for those elements that I knew to be challenging or prone to error – usually where there were difficult fluids involved or high degrees of interaction with the work of other engineering disciplines. This worked well and we made few, if any, mistakes and we didn't waste time.

APL was a very satisfactory company to work in; it was big enough to have a pretty full range of resources and expertise, but small enough that everyone had an identifiable, important role.

Over the years, as the company grew from being a middle sized organisation to a large one, more and more procedures were introduced. We moved from a culture in which well-experienced engineers took responsibility for their own work to one in which many individuals were in a hurry to broaden their experience and move up the organisation. Also, because they were somewhat transient and inexperienced, they would expect someone else to check their work – and take responsibility for it. This was a trend of the industry and not only of my company. It did produce people with a broad understanding of the business, but reliable work-horse engineers became fewer and fewer. Appraisals and remuneration began to recognise potential and not good, solid competence and hard work. The result was more mistakes and lower efficiency – checking will never catch all errors, it dilutes responsibility and adds a lot of unproductive work.

In modern quality management, parlance checking and other quality control functions are the "cost of conformance", while errors and the necessary correction work are the "cost of non-conformance". I saw both costs steadily increase as the company grew. Some of my colleagues referred to the engineering content of our work as the meat in the sandwich and we watched as the bread became thicker and the meat thinner in a big, corporate, global organisation.

Something I have learned in life is that extreme views and opinions are likely to be damaging; it is not that checking and procedures are bad – they can be effective if they help to record and make available good practice – but they can be carried to excess and reduce quality and efficiency when they are imposed by administrators who do not fully understand the work. An example of this is in planning. Most companies now have planning specialists and you can even hire planning consultants. Such people soon come to believe that planning is an end in itself and imagine that multi-coloured charts and tables of data somehow add value. They believe that a "planning system" can be equally applied to all engineering disciplines and readily discount the differences in job content between, say, an electrical engineer and a piping designer.

I have seen effective planning practices of individual groups and section heads swept away and replaced by corporately inspired universal systems that provide "management information" (actually the information the planning experts think managers need rather than what they actually need), adding unproductive work, reducing the control and effectiveness of those executing the work and, often, reducing the judgement and effectiveness of managers.

Later in my career, when I had reached a senior engineering management position, I developed tools to measure the efficiency of engineering design work. I had begun to use these to inform my decisions as a manager, just as the corporate desire for a global organisation really gathered momentum. I was making steady progress improving work processes and quality, but this was swept away by enthusiastic Americans who believed so strongly in what was being done in America that they had no interest in good practices in other parts of the company.

Later, after ten years of "globalisation", I used my measurement tools again and found that we were using 30% more hours to do the same work. On top of this were added costs due to errors and delays.

In my more senior positions I became closer to the business and developed some understanding of what our competitors were doing. I watched with some envy as our principal German competitor, Linde, became more effective. One of the reasons for this was their approach to globalisation; they seemed to have strong, semi-autonomous regional organisations coupled with effective coordination of the parts. One example was their purchasing organisation. When they sought out lower cost suppliers in developing regions, they used their local organisations in which people were able to speak the same language as the manufacturers and engage the local market with credibility. It was obvious that we would not induce serious responses from potential suppliers when we sent enquiries in English from America or the UK and imposed the Laws of Pennsylvania.

There were some negatives, but many good things about APL. There was a strong emphasis on the development, support and respect of its people; ability and performance were more important than qualifications or connections and there was an ethical approach to business.

This encouraged a strong work ethic and attracted able people who were stimulating to work with. It was a good company; it could have been great if the Americans could have brought their positive qualities and allowed more consideration of what the British and other parts of the company could offer. Overall I felt the combination of American management and British engineers was a strong one. The American culture and education system do produce strong management, but British engineers tend to be more innovative and technically stronger.

Although it would change significantly in later years, at that time APL was not as good as the Gas Board at employing handicapped people. I had two experiences of trying to hire people with a minor disability. They both had excellent technical experience and ability. One was a man who had recovered from kidney disease. Although he had made a complete recovery, advice from the company doctor was that he had a higher risk than normal of kidney problems in the future and it would affect our health insurance costs. The personnel department vetoed his appointment. The other man had only one arm. The personnel manager again blocked the application saying that, in his experience, such people had a chip on the shoulder and could be difficult. He hadn't noticed the irony in his remark.

My promotion to the first tier of management had come a little too soon and Edward had come a little too soon, but I needed to grasp the opportunities before me.

I worked on my degree, attending the Poly for a day and an evening and I did at least ten hours' home study each week. This necessitated giving up all other home activities: home improvements, gardening and watching television. It was fantastic for Rosie to have supported me in this when there was so much to do on the house. She carried the major workload of the children and home and managed in a Dickensian kitchen.

For much of the time I moved to the shed where I had installed a desk. The children would visit me and my degree notes became embellished with their crayoned additions. It seemed easier to let them scribble while I concentrated on my studies.

In April, Argentinean forces invaded the Falkland Islands and my daily routine, after getting home from work, was to do at least two hours' study before the nine o'clock news when I could allow myself the luxury of watching the daily update. Margaret Thatcher had started her premiership with her ridiculous Francis of Assisi speech and it was then we knew we had a mad woman in charge. However, her handling of the war was impeccable and then we knew why she had been elected. It was destiny; she was in the job just for that moment in history that needed a single minded, uncompromising and belligerent response to Argentinean aggression.

I loved doing the degree work. To study for an engineering degree with already 15 years' experience in engineering was wonderful. So many times I was said to myself, "I've always wanted to know how to do this or that calculation." I was the perfect, conscientious student; no more the scrape-through-with-40% approach of my earlier studies. I was one of only three students to achieve a commendation pass and I also carried away the Institution of Mechanical Engineers' academic prize for my final year project – that had been in competition with all part-time and full time students in the Poly.

Rosie and I had done it and I had an education at last. The mental gymnastics of my studies had sharpened my ability to use the little grey cells; it was like having a brain transplant and I could see everything more clearly, not just engineering science and mathematics, but every day and business activities.

I was the first person on my mother's side of the family and the second on my dad's (my cousin Carol, whom I hardly knew had qualified as a vet), to get a degree. Rosie and Mum attended the degree award ceremony with me. Rosie stood back as Mum joined me for the official "family" graduation photograph. My wife, who had made this possible, was content that all the work had achieved the desired result. My mother, for whom I was the vicarious success she had worked and hoped for, needed to be in the centre of the celebration and then she would return to her widow's life. Rosie and I did not discuss this; we just did what seemed to be right. It was usually like that with us. We did not need to discuss things like having children, house moves, career moves or holiday plans; we had similar aspirations, energy levels and risk appetites.

The degree meant a lot to this stupid country boy who needed it to prove to himself what had been hoped for – that he could do it, that the opportunity for education that existed in our liberal democracy could be tapped by an 11+ failure who had been conditioned to be satisfied with a subordinate place below those born to privilege. Yes, I had a chip on the shoulder, but now I understood it and could live with it.

My degree gave me confidence and, possibly because it was fresher than the education of my peers, I had a better grip on mathematics and engineering science than most of them. I was able to overhaul some of our calculation methods and write new engineering standards for systems that were challenging to design. An example of this was the design of compressor anti-surge control systems that need cross-discipline coordination involving Process, Machinery, Piping and Instrument Engineers. Prior to that many of our designs had not worked first time and had to be modified in the field.

I also wrote articles on cryogenic control valve design and safety valve sizing and selection for the Institute of Chemical Engineers' journal and I sat on the steering committee for the production of the Institute's Relief Systems Handbook.

When the company's lease on the office block in New Malden had come to an end in 1981, it was decided that the time was right to own an office building and we moved to new offices in Hersham. This was an additional bonus; I now had an easy half hour drive to work.

We also needed to think about building at home. With three bedrooms and four children, more space was needed. We would have liked to have extended and modernised the kitchen as well as adding a bedroom and a family room and had plans drawn up. Quotations were obtained from builders. The kitchen part of the plan would cost nearly as much as the two-storey bedroom and family room and we could only afford one part. We borrowed a further £8000 and went ahead with the two-storey extension in 1982, gaining the space we really needed.

When my degree was finished, I set about the kitchen, stealing a bit from the hallway to increase its size and fitting it out with new cupboards and sink. It was not ideal but it was serviceable.

The interest rate on our mortgage had been high, but it got worse. We had almost no disposable income and could balance our books only with great care. For a few months in the summer, I cycled the 15 miles to work on Dad's old Raleigh bicycle. This was all fine; we were a strong family unit with a great deal to be thankful for. All it needed was hard work and perseverance and we were capable of that.

Chapter 17

On the Ladder

It was around this time that I made a business trip to Cairo to see if we could sell an air separation plant to the steel company. This was a short trip of only a few days, but it gave me a fascinating peep into another world.

I stayed in a luxurious hotel, once the palace of Empress Eugenie, wife of Napoleon III, who visited Cairo for the opening of the Suez Canal in 1869. My room overlooked the Nile. I could see a few of the open boats from which fishermen plied their trade, casting nets into the brown water. These were traditional wooden craft, probably inherited from the father and each boat accommodated not only the fisherman and his nets, but his family also. His wife sat at the rear with a stove perched on the transom preparing food, while the children kept out of the way in the bow; I suppose keeping out of the way until they were old enough to help with the fishing.

At this point the river divided into two channels and I could look down on an impressive iron bridge, the Abu-el-Ella Bridge. It was a bridge of some complexity and my enquiries led to the information that it had been designed by Gustave Eiffel, also responsible for the structure of the Statue of Liberty on Statton Island (1886), the well known tower built for the Exposition Universelle in Paris (1889), as well as buildings and bridges all over the world. The bridge was designed to open to allow the passage of river traffic. It opened and closed just once before jamming. My local informant had it that the disappointment was too much for Eiffel to bear, leading to his suicide by hanging on the bridge.

The record tells that this is not correct and that Eiffel died of natural causes at his home in Paris in 1923, although it is also recorded that he suffered from depression and may, indeed, have eventually taken his own life, but not on the Abu-el-Ella Bridge.

Both the statue and the bridge had been intended to promote French interests around the world and outdo the British. An inherited antipathy for the French, brewed from generations of rivalry of the two empires, leads me unable to resist a little satisfaction in a French failure. The statue may have been partially successful, but the bridge must have had the opposite effect, reminding Cairo of French engineering incompetence, as it stood there impeding river navigation for nearly a hundred years. It was eventually demolished in 1998.

When my driver took me to the steel works, a drive of about ten miles south along the Nile, we first navigated the city roads. These were roads, but pedestrians seemed to take precedence and it was stop-and-go as the route was "negotiated". Shortly after leaving the hotel, we had to wait for pedestrians to cross in front of us. Following a group of men, a solitary individual with no arms and one leg hopped cheerfully across while his companions walked nonchalantly on their way.

Ten minutes later we were leaving the suburbs. We had passed occasional sand-bagged security posts manned by armed soldiers and, at one point, a platoon of them marched along the road in pairs. Each soldier on the left carried his rifle on his left shoulder and each one on the right carried his on his right shoulder. This arrangement allowed each pair to hold hands; a comical sight to someone unfamiliar with Arab culture.

Leaving the city we joined a dual carriageway, or what was left of it. The driver said that the road had been built by the British; this would date it prior to 1956 when Egypt attained full independence from Britain following the Suez crisis. It was very apparent that it had not been maintained by anyone for many years. Large potholes impeded progress and, in some places where one carriageway was impassable, we simply bumped over what was left of the central reservation and continued south on the northbound carriageway, dodging on-coming traffic. I had been in some interesting situations and had travelled with Italian taxi drivers on my travels, but on this journey, I got past worrying about my safety and abandoned myself to fate. At last I saw the great iron gates of the steel works come into view and I knew Allah had been with me. The gates were open and the driver aimed for the space between them. As if determined to make the journey eventful, he crashed into one of the gates, but we bounced off, unhurt, with just another dent in the minibus.

I was in a delegation of three, led by our business manager and supported by our Egyptian agent and a representative of the German company who would bring their experience of working in Egypt to a partnership with us if we were successful. Later, over drinks, I gained the impression that their expertise was mainly their willingness to identify and bribe someone in the steel company's management team to sponsor our bid. This would not give us any advantage, but would get our bid accepted; it was just the cost of doing business in this place. We were an ethical company and could not be involved in "under the table" activities, but we could work with a partner with local knowledge!

I was learning management skills through experience and realised I needed to move on from behaving as a lead engineer to being a leader of my group.

One of the jobs I was still doing myself was the sizing and selection of pressure safety valves. This had always been considered a black art that needed years of experience. It did need a lot of experience and knowledge to engineer these important safety devices properly, but we were always dealing with the same fluids at the same sort of conditions and I wondered if we could automate the design process. I had a bright, but arrogant graduate assigned to my group and I had a few complaints about his attitude from the people in other departments. He was low on charm, but he did know how to programme the office computer in its Fortran language. I worked with him to analyse the work process and decision points in the safety valve black art and he produced a successful programme to do the job. The senior engineer's task of sizing and selecting pressure safety valves became a job for a junior and the verification of his (it was always "his" at this time) work would be only to check that the right data had been entered into the computer. This programme was used for many years and was a significant efficiency improvement. Again, it was pretty much a local innovation.

A little later, when our American masters decided we needed to be a "global" company, they would "launch" new ideas from head office on us with great enthusiasm and individuals would receive much credit and esteem for their improvements, which would be measured in hours and costs saved and they would be rewarded through the global appraisal system. If all the hours and money claimed to have been saved were added up, the calculation would have revealed that a new plant could be engineered with no hours and at no cost. This was one American practice that tended to be viewed with distain by us in the UK, especially since innovations originating in our "backward" satellite office would not usually be of much interest to the global company.

This was partially due to the difference in the education systems and culture and Americans were simply better at selling where we seemed to feel, usually to our own disadvantage, that that sort of behaviour was beneath us and we would rather just get on with the job.

The 1979 general election saw the election of our first woman Prime Minister. Some trade union activists were unwilling to moderate the crusade and the NUM elected Arthur Scargill as their president. He was just the man to take on another Tory Prime Minister, but seemed not to notice that coal stocks were building up sufficiently to withstand a long conflict. He ran right into it and gave Mrs. Thatcher the mandate to kill the mining industry and she felt no need to facilitate alternative employment for the communities that depended on it. Her right hand Rottweiler, Norman Tebbit, advised them to "get on their bikes."

1984, the year of the miners' strike, when 27 million days were lost, was to be the last year of widespread industrial chaos. With the unions broken, we would see many years with an absence of strike action and time lost to strike action decreased steadily and significantly. Just over 20 years later, in 2005, there would be 156,000 working days lost, the lowest calendar year total since comparable records began in 1891.

Well, industrial relations improved, but only when there was no longer industry to have relations in; what a crude and primitive solution. These uncompromising Conservative policies could work to some extent if we could vaporise those put out of work, but if we consider them to be people who need to be housed and fed, to educate their children and look after their aged, then putting them out of work with no planned alternative is not very practical.

The aspect of elitist Conservative policy that affected our family was the withdrawal of funding from education. I don't think I realised it at the time, but Comprehensive schools were struggling to provide the education that the nation aspired to in the 1980s.

Margaret Thatcher had set about reducing public spending and, by the mid 1980s, this had brought state education to a very low level with school buildings in poor condition and teachers underpaid and undervalued. Esteem in the profession was low and many, if not most, children were leaving school with attainments far below their potential. Some teachers continued to do their best, but others became militant and some developed back problems and other mysterious maladies that enabled them to play truant.

After years of good labour relations under both Conservative and Labour governments, a new Conservative government, in 2010, would again see a major union, the National Union of Teachers, calling strike action. There are many advantages to living in a liberal democracy and we are making progress towards a fairer society in which more people have the opportunity to reach their potential, but it is frustrating that the pendulum politics that goes with it are so crude and disadvantage those caught in the wrong part of the cycle.

Our older children were disadvantaged by the Thatcher years, coming as they did at the critical point in their education. They were bright enough to achieve sufficient A-levels to get them to university, but they received little guidance on how to reach their potential.

We were attending the United Reformed Church regularly. With our children, the Kellys and several other families, there was an active junior church. We ran a youth club that met weekly, organised week long holiday activities and went on a few hikes, camping overnight.

There was no red tape; we just did it and welcomed whatever help was offered. I am sure the child protection regulations that were later put into force help to safeguard our children, but it was much easier at this time and we could channel all our effort into the activities without an administrative overhead.

I found the Sunday morning church services offered me a reflective interval, a calm oasis, in my busy week and, in the URC, dogma was much less important than the intellectual and spiritual parts of religion. I was gradually becoming a Christian. There has been no epiphany, just a slow leaking away of objections and a growing appreciation of the spiritual and social dimensions of being involved with a church family; a family of those in the community who chose to share in it.

Process instrumentation was still predominantly pneumatic, but the development of computers had been progressed for sequential operations, especially in mechanical handling operations in other industries. I had been monitoring these developments and I thought the functionality and robustness of these programmable logic controllers could be approaching what we would need. I investigated and tested a couple of the best I could find. I was particularly impressed with a unit made by the Texas Instrument Company (TI): the PM550. This had both logic and analogue control processors and was very well built. TI loaned me a system and I taught myself to programme it. It could provide all the automation we needed for a small nitrogen plant and I decided to go ahead.

As I have said, we in APL were quite autonomous in those days and I had a free hand. However, I could imagine that there could be concern about moving into computer control in our industry, so I was careful to call my new system a "multi-function controller" and not a "computer".

As a precaution, I engineered a back-up panel so the plant could still be operated if the computer should not be sufficiently reliable. In the event, the computer was superb and I did not install back-up panels on the plants that followed. I was very satisfied with this piece of clandestine innovation.

The company was growing and so was my group. I had a few long term experienced engineers, but we were also attracting increasing numbers of young graduates. We managed to create an atmosphere in which both experience and youthful vigour were respected and Instrument Design became the group of choice for our graduate trainees. I offered them a deal: they would work their socks off for me and I would do what I could to help them move on in their careers. 15 years later most managers in Engineering and a Senior Vice President would have spent their formative years with me. Included in this successful group was the arrogant graduate with Fortran knowledge who had quickly come to understand the importance of inter-personal skills and had completely revised his. I imagined, and hoped, that I would find myself working for him one day. Although he became very able, that I never did was probably more due to circumstances and not to any shortage of ability on his part.

Some of the engineering graduates were women and the first of these needed us to make quite a bit of adjustment. I had all the girly calendars taken down. There were a few cycles of them reappearing and being removed, but the new order was soon accepted. A slightly more difficult change was our language. It had been understood that engineering communication had to be punctuated with expletives and you couldn't make yourself understood by a Piping Designer without the "f" word.

Rachael joined the group and we worked on our personal development. It wasn't that Rachael demanded or expected a change, but somehow we just thought it would be right. It was not easy at first, but gradually we discovered that the English language had many words available and, indeed, it was possible to work successfully while being polite and respectful. We continued to shelter Rachael from visiting Piping Designers, but eventually this step in social evolution was essentially complete. It had increased our self esteem and our effectiveness.

Soon I had more women in my group than there were in any other part of the Engineering Department. For a while this brought another advantage: it was that I could send one of my lady engineers to lead a particularly difficult negotiation and, while women were still something of a novelty in our industry, they would usually be successful. I

190

would advise them to cry if the negotiation was going badly, but I don't think any of them ever did this.

Chapter 18

All Zis Bullshit

Each year I would have a development plan to which all members of the group would contribute. Everyone seemed to grow in ability and confidence and it worked well for a few years. I was given responsibility for the Electrical Engineering group and we became the Electrical and Controls Department with a manager and three Section Heads for electrical, instrumentation and controls. There was opportunity for an individual to progress within the department or to move to another. After a time, however, I realised that I needed to move to make way for one of my Section Heads to grow into my job. This was to keep faith with a principle I had come to believe was important: to allow headroom for those ambitious to advance their careers.

I gave up my position, took an assignment as a Project Manager and led a project to build a new plant engineered in Hersham and built in Alabama. This was not a promotion, but it did enable me to gain experience of project management. I was again working directly with Americans and this was enjoyable; with their work ethic, openness and sincerity they can be very good colleagues. America is a very big country and Alabama with its wide open spaces is very different to the Eastern Seaboard of New York and Pennsylvania.

On one business trip, I arrived at the Holiday Inn in Decatur, Alabama. I had planned to meet colleagues from the T-town office for dinner, but they did not arrive until the next day. It transpired that their travel office had booked them to Decatur, Illinois!

I admire the positive attitude of many American engineers. Our construction superintendent on the site was from Texas. He owned a ranch and was a rodeo rider when he didn't need to be earning real money. He wore cowboy boots, blue jeans and a large belt buckle. When there were problems he would simply set about solving them; no thought wasted on whose fault it might be, just effort to move forward. If there was a bigger problem, I observed he would come to work the next day with an even bigger belt buckle and, invigorated by this talisman, would overcome all obstacles.

After the Decatur project, I moved back into engineering management, this time leading the plant design group, which included civil, structural, piping and stress engineering and design functions and the support facilities such as printing and document management. I had enjoyed a great technical interest in my work on instrumentation and controls, but now it felt good to be free from direct technical responsibility and to be able to concentrate on management – creating an environment in which the whole team could reach its potential.

The engineering activities were grouped under me and two other managers who led machinery engineering and my old electrical and controls department. The other significant group in engineering was the project management department. Most of the senior project managers were experienced, but did not seem to be adapting well to the changing scale and challenges of our business. The other two engineering managers and I adopted the practice of meeting regularly to ensure that the work of our departments was well coordinated. We did much of the project manager's work for them, probably without them realising.

I would have been happy to stay in the engineering management role for a lot longer, but after a couple of years the company undertook a large and complicated project to build a very large hydrogen plant with integrated heat and power production in Pernis in Rotterdam's Europort area. I was directed to take the role of senior project manager leading this. This was fine; I was a resource to be used to support the company's business. Project management is largely common sense, but it does need a lot of experience to avoid the many pitfalls that are waiting to make life difficult. I was responsible for a hundred million dollars of investment and I needed to work very hard for long hours to keep it under control. One aspect of project management that I did not understand was currency management and, unfortunately, nobody alerted me to the basic disciplines I should follow.

The project was financed in Dutch guilders and I later discovered it was my responsibility to advise the treasury department to "hedge" the other currencies we would need to spend. I failed to call for the sterling hedge and the guilder rapidly increased in value over a short period. Currency movements are like this – stable for long periods then sudden changes. My incompetence made a profit of just over a million pounds. This sounds fine, but it could just as easily have been a loss and, had that been the case, my project management career might have been much shorter.

At that time we had a forceful and charismatic managing director, an East German who had escaped to the west and built a successful career. I had heard that he was forthright and plain speaking, but I didn't see much wrong with that. As the project manager of our biggest project, it fell to me to visit Ad Becker and give him an update on the progress of the project. The first time I was invited to his inner sanctum I was feeling particularly enthusiastic. The project was going well and we had done some good engineering.

I imagined Ad would be interested in the details and, when invited to give an update, I proceeded to explain exactly how the civil engineers had re-engineered the table top foundations of the redundant compressors to be able to accept the new alternators[3]. With the completely different machine dynamics, it would have been likely that complete demolition and replacement would have been required, but some very clever work had avoided the expense and time this would have cost. Well, I hadn't noticed Ad getting frustrated with all this engineering talk. I think he had tried to be polite (not one of his strengths), but had finally had enough and exploded. "Vas is all zis bullshit? Ver are zee costs? Cost, I wan' zee costs!" I showed him the costs and retreated. I guess I had the wrong focus and this is probably why I would never be the MD.

I worked through the Pernis project, recalibrating my knowledge of engineering management as I went. There were many challenges and I needed to work hard and for long hours. In the second year of the project, in September, I noticed that, apart from a week for the family holiday, I had not taken a weekend off since January. There were many dimensions and it was very absorbing. On the technical side, we were taking a 25-year-old ammonia plant, keeping and refurbishing the reformer, steam turbines and utilities parts, demolishing the ammonia synthesis loop, replacing its compressors with alternators to generate 25 kilo-Watts of electricity and adding new adsorption equipment. This was to produce pure hydrogen to supply the Esso refinery as it upgraded its processes to make low sulphur fuels that would meet the requirement of the new European legislation.

Refurbishing an old plant is always challenging because you cannot be certain the condition of the equipment is fully understood, but in this case we had bought the plant from another company and we had no experience of it; they had shut it down and retired the staff. I kept a souvenir hanging on the wall of my office. It was a small section of

---

[3]The design of the foundations has to consider the vibrations of the machine over its entire starting and operating range to ensure sufficient damping at the harmonic frequencies.

rust-perforated steel that had been part of the brackish cooling water supply pipe to the plant's cooling systems. It was an underground line 150 metres long, 1 metre diameter and 12 mm thick. According to my budget it was in good condition and needed no work. Well, it needed complete replacement; a big hole in the ground, with all the disruption and a big hole in my finances.

Managing projects in an operating company has some real professional advantages; you work closely with the operations team and learn, through feedback, a lot about the technology. This is very satisfying. The downside is that the scope, for which there is a fixed budget, tends to grow to include everything that is needed to complete the work to the satisfaction of the operations group. I had great admiration for our operations group; they consistently achieved exceptional reliability and performance. They were conscientious about sharing feedback and insisting on good practice in the design and construction of our plants. This did add cost, a lot of cost and could make us uncompetitive because it was so hard to know which enhancements really did contribute to the good performance.

I discovered another hole in my budget. When we commenced the project, we were allowed a cooling water effluent temperature into the harbour of 35 degrees C. For political reasons, the Dutch government wanted to buy French nuclear generated electricity, but they had a law prohibiting import unless the Dutch generating capacity was insufficient. Well, a good way to make it "insufficient" was to limit the allowable effluent temperature to 30 C.

This would necessitate the Dutch power stations, reducing load. My plant would have to reduce load also, or invest in an atmospheric cooling system – at a cost of several million pounds. Turning down capacity was not an option because we had a contract with Esso.

Europort was our biggest concentration of investment in the world. There were several large plants and they were quite interdependent. Any passing project was considered fair game by the operations team, to slip in any enhancements they wanted to fund, or any maintenance that might be paid for by a project. The possibilities were endless and this project manager's minefield was known as "the Rozenburg factor". Rozenburg was the town nearest to the centre of our group of plants. You might find you were paying for a new 5 mile long water supply pipe, a new electrical sub-station or noise abatement for the whole facility – and there was an army of dedicated experts waiting to pounce.

There were business and cultural considerations. It appeared that local engineering contractors operated a cartel in the Europort area. I was told the procedure went like this.

A contractor would go to the contractors' association and "claim" a contract when he had grounds for doing this and you had to be careful about "engaging the market" as you prepared for a project. If you later requested competitive bids from a number of contractors, the contractor who had successfully claimed the work would increase his bid to cover the bidding costs of all the contractors and the other bidders would offer an even higher price. If you had asked for, say, six bids, the premium would be 10 or 15%. This mafia had a pretty good understanding of the complicated Dutch labour laws and they had effective control of local construction infrastructure, such as concrete supplies and this may have contributed to their grip on the local business.

When government contracts were "nobbled" in this way there were prosecutions, but I don't think the shady practices were completely eliminated.

Added to this, the Dutch are formidable negotiators. They are never confused by facts or reasonableness; they

198

are never embarrassed by their own failings. They consider everything they can get away with to be good business. I saw a quotation of George Canning who was a 19th century British Prime Minister. He wrote, in a coded letter, Jan. 31, 1826, to the English ambassador at The Hague, Holland: "In matters of commerce the fault of the Dutch is offering too little and asking too much."

In my experience the Dutch have not changed in 180 years. Every detail has to be negotiated and cannot be concluded until you have conceded enough to the Dutchman to let him feel he has hurt you. The effect of this is that you have to start from a position that allows for this movement. By contrast, Americans are generally straightforward to deal with; you can immediately put a deal on the table that provides advantage for both sides. If you have assessed it correctly, the American will just agree; a so called win-win situation.

For all these vicissitudes, the Dutch are thorough and skilful and, outside work, they can be good company. I enjoyed staying in the local family run hotels. The Dutch embrace modern technology, but they are old-fashioned in some comfortable, homely ways and these hotels made a welcome change from the sterile American and European chain organisations. One particular establishment in Oostvoorne was run by two brothers and their wives. One of the women was a real dragon and would admonish the guests for any unacceptable behaviour, such as being late for dinner. And the food was just what was needed; simple home cooking.

Another lesson I learned on that project was about consultants; you can never rely on a consultant. Sometimes you are obliged to employ a local consultant to facilitate building and environmental permits. They understand the local rules, know the decision makers in the local authority and speak the language. Many are professional and can provide a good service. However, by the nature of the way their services are contracted for, they have little or no stake in achieving schedule or cost targets and they love additional work. They will have the expertise you need – that is why you selected them – but they will assign an unsupervised trainee to your work and you will not know that they are missing all the scheduled dates unless you monitor them very closely. It has to be like supervising a child with no opportunity given for slippage or deviation. The defined scope of the Pernis project was executed within its budget and schedule. However, there had been many scope additions and I had been unable to secure cost coverage for all of them. From the senior management perspective, I had failed as a project manager and my reputation was damaged sufficiently with my American masters to slow the progress of my career, at least for a couple of years. The plant was initially a great success, however, and ran for 540 days without an interruption. World class performance for a new plant of this type would have been around four interruptions a year, more in the first year as teething troubles were sorted out.

From the point of view of senior management, who are informed by the business management group, the project was over budget. For an internal project – one in which we were building a plant for company ownership and operation – there was no one else to pay the bills and the "contract" between the engineering and operating parts of the company would be somewhat fluid.

The business managers would see the budget as fixed, but the scope of work could vary to ensure the projected financial returns could be achieved. Occasionally there could be tension between these groups: Engineering, Operations and Business.

On one occasion, Gerry Browne, the senior business manager for the Benelux area, which included Rotterdam, had made some erroneous statements about the direction of another Rotterdam project and, as the senior Engineering manager, I needed to explain why his preferred situation was not achievable. I made an appointment to meet him in his Rotterdam office. This manager was an American who was moving up in his career with the expectation of an eventual board position and, at that time, was gathering the required experience of the company's business in Europe.

"I'm rather busy," he explained when I telephoned, "but I could see you for a few minutes at 11am before I go to an appointment in Breda."

Well, I arrived at 10.50am and sipped a cup of coffee while I waited. Browne arrived; his secretary brought him coffee.

"I've only got a few minutes, but we can deal with our business."

"Thank you for seeing me Gerry; it will be useful to clear up the misunderstanding," and, looking for a diplomatic way of putting my point of view, I said, "I can understand why you would take the view you have, Gerry."

Seeing his opportunity, Browne jumped out of his chair and grabbed his coat, making for the door.

"I'm so pleased we agree," he said as he disappeared. "Must go; just time to get to Breda."

He was gone. Breda at this hour meant a nice business lunch with his Exxon customer. And he was able to report that he and I had discussed the project and agreed.

Browne, a more down to earth American colleague advised me, was a "Preppie" – he had been educated at Princeton. This made him the American equivalent of an English public school toff and he behaved in the same manipulative way as you can frequently experience in Britain. The class system in America is less rigid than in Britain, but it does exist and people know their place, especially if their place is near the top of the heap.

Browne had successfully outflanked me. I could only console myself that I had the moral high ground. Browne didn't care much about that.

The next time I had occasion to work with Browne, it was to help him with a customer meeting in The Hague by providing the engineering credibility.

"Could you fly over to Schipol? I'll meet you and we can have a bit of lunch, then visit the customer to explain our capability. It's early days in building the relationship and this customer isn't available for lunch."

The Hague I thought. Good restaurants in The Hague I thought. I was busy, but it's important to support the business, especially when there's a good lunch in it.

Browne was at the arrivals' gate to meet me.

"The car's in the short stay, but we've time for a bite."

Before I could respond, he marched me to the airport Burger King and offered me anything on the menu. Thanks Gerry; nice to do business with you.

My second Browne lesson: I was not the class of person that you needed to entertain to a restaurant lunch.

Chapter 19

A Late Developer

Hydrogen was becoming important business and the company organised its engineering support into two groups: one to serve the more traditional air separation technologies and the other the hydrogen and carbon monoxide technologies. After the Pernis project, I became the manager responsible for all hydrogen and carbon monoxide (HyCO) projects. This work embraced high temperature reforming, adsorption and cryogenic technologies and was interesting, as was the business: working with customers and suppliers to formulate, execute and hand over major process plants in many countries around the world.

Project management is just common sense, backed up by commercial awareness and a good knowledge of the technologies, an understanding of engineering processes, information flow, management of change, safety, quality, schedule, cost, contracts and people. It is usually absorbing, but can be tedious. An aim should be to avoid excitement; keep life simple. The project manager also has to do everything no one else wants to do, including technical interfaces between engineering disciplines, obtaining permits, applying for grants, document management and transport.

Although I had not planned a career in project management, I found it challenging and satisfying and, for me, it was made possible by my years of experience in operations, design and construction engineering that gave me a grasp of the logistics of getting things done in an engineering environment. I observed that engineers often move into project management for the wrong reasons.

Commonly, they have high energy, but lack the ability to concentrate on the detail needed in an engineering discipline and they imagine life will be easier if they "de-specialise". However, like design engineering, project management requires concentration, coupled with a clear head and the tenacity to follow all activities through to completion. I think this is why so many seemed to be from the Genghis Khan school and resorted to bluster and bullying in a desperate attempt to get things done when they have not done the ground work.

I felt I was making a contribution. I was in a job I enjoyed, using the skills I had developed over the years and working with people I respected. Also, I felt that Britain was in the best condition ever. We had a government with a balanced view; committed to social improvement and supportive of business.

Tony Blair had been elected with the biggest majority since the war. After the enormous social advances initiated by Clement Atlee's post-war government, other Labour governments had been a disappointment. With the possible exception of Harold Wilson, leaders had been well intentioned idealists who had not understood that the country needed to be run on sound business lines. Trades unions, essential to give a voice to workers views and aspirations, had been corrupted by people pursuing a left wing political agenda. Conservative governments had confronted union power, culminating in Margaret Thatcher's government, which had curbed union excesses but this had been at the expense of wrecking Britain's industrial base.

In my role as Manager of Projects for HyCO, I needed to do more travel in support of the development of business opportunities. One such trip took me with two colleagues to western China, to a chemical works on the Yangtze River near the city of Chongqing in the Sichuan province.

204

This involved an internal flight from Beijing to Chongqing and a ride over mountains on gravel roads in a truck. The internal flight was interesting. After I had squeezed into my seat with Chinese legroom, I began to notice the poor state of repair of the seats and cabin fixtures. Did this level of engineering diligence extend to the airframe and engines? After a couple of hours in the air, an announcement was made in Chinese. This was followed, thoughtfully, by a truncated English translation for the three Europeans, "Radies and gentremen, we have a probrem." This was not reassuring, but it transpired that the steward did not know the English for "air turbulence".

The truck ride was uncomfortable but uneventful. I had learned to decipher some of the Chinese characters on road signs. On bends in this rough dirt and gravel track, where there was an opportunity to leave the road and plunge down the mountain side, there would usually be a sign indicating the number of men who had met such a fate.

At a small town en route we stopped for a meal. The restaurant was just a concrete shell with a room accommodating two round tables and another serving as a kitchen. I was to learn that eating in this area was a team effort. Our translator ordered for us and, presently, a washing-up bowl full of dirty water with a dead fish floating in it was placed in the centre of the table. The method of eating was to hold the fish with your chopsticks while a colleague pulled off a bit of flesh and ate it. He would then return the favour. It was pretty unappetising and probably not enhanced, because when I had asked to wash my hands, had been led through the "kitchen" to the tap on the outside wall. The kitchen I passed through was filthy and people were preparing our food on the floor. If it had not been for a need to make polite observance of the customs and accept offers of food, I would have happily lived off the supply of Mars bars I carried in my suitcase.

At the chemical works we found a modern and reasonably maintained facility comprised of 20 or so plants. It appeared to be a self contained enterprise with its own farm land, a shoe factory and schools as well as workshops for the fabrication of pressure vessels. The engineers we met were knowledgeable and we had constructive meetings, which lasted a couple of days. The weather was very hot and humid. Just standing outside would have skin dripping with perspiration in ten minutes with no exertion at all.

On the last evening, the head man held a banquet for us. The food served was quite different from the anything else we had experienced in Sichuan – dozens of different dishes, served by young ladies dressed in a smart traditional Chinese style. Our hosts seemed to be trying to shock us with the "delicacy" of their local cuisine. They brought frogs legs – hoping for a reaction – but were disappointed when we responded by saying we had frogs legs all the time at home. They did, however, get the reaction they wanted with "pig's neck nerve". At least this is the translation they gave to the egg sized rubber brain-like objects they served in sweet sauce. With chop sticks these could not be cut and, we learned, with teeth they couldn't be chewed with any decrease in their elasticity. We just had to swallow and hope that our weakened digestive juices would break down this indestructible substance in a few weeks.

It had, again, been good to meet and work with engineers in another land. I exited China with only a mild dose of dysentery and, again, the trip home felt like the end of a tough campaign.

As I built my team, project engineers were assigned to me from other parts of the company. I soon realised that those people who were "available" were the ones their managers didn't want.

This didn't matter because most were able and just needed a little support and the opportunity to show their capabilities.

One of my new staff was a German. He was intelligent and industrious, but he was a troubled soul. One of the endearing things about him, however, was that he never seemed to understand the British sense of humour. He had observed it over the 10 years he had lived in England. Well, what he had observed was that Englishmen would talk nonsense, then laugh. All irony, build-up and language subtlety was missed; Klaus would sometimes talk nonsense, then wait for the approving laughter that, of course, never materialised.

The company culture encouraged the development of its people and an interesting personal development exercise we were all encouraged to participate in was Myers-Briggs personality profiling. This would tell you what sort of person you were according to four character attributes – introversion (I); extraversion (E); sensing (S); intuition (N); thinking (T); feeling (F); judgment (J) and perception (P). It transpired that most Air Products senior managers were ISTJ – analytical and judgmental rather than intuitive and emotional. Before participating in this, I had assumed that those who disagreed with me were just not concentrating – not using the available data effectively. After seeing the results and comparing my profile with others, I was convinced I had been right. At last I understood why some people failed to come to the right conclusions!

There was some gender influence in the results, with women tending to be intuitive and emotional (touchy-feely). When Klaus got his results he was relieved to find he was touchy-feely. He had always thought he was a woman and this was the confirmation he wanted.

I had noticed Klaus wearing clear nail varnish, but had assumed this was a German thing. Also, at a recent meeting, the general manager for Engineering had remarked, "Your hair is getting long Klaus. I don't like to see my project managers with long hair. Get it cut."

Klaus didn't get it cut; he came into my office a couple of days later and reported that he had been receiving medical help and his problem had been diagnosed: he was suffering from "gender dysphoria". I received the information coolly, because I didn't know what it meant. If you are thinking about budgets and reformer tubes and someone comes along and blurts out that they are suffering from "gender dysphoria", it might take a few moments to re-calibrate your reference points. Anyway, Klaus was apparently relieved that I had not reacted badly. Although I rarely discussed my personal life at work, Klaus had the (correct) impression that I was a Christian and, further, the impression that Christians are intolerant of transsexuals.

Klaus' condition was one I didn't understand, but I took it seriously that someone could be so disorientated that they felt they needed treatment. He was clearly going through a very difficult time and a sympathetic response would be appropriate. During the "treatment" process, Klaus became Katrin and said she felt much happier.

Klaus and I had worked together to build a hydrogen plant on Teesside. I was generally very happy with Klaus' efforts as Project Manager. He was thoroughly conscientious and disciplined; he controlled costs and managed the work well until the construction fell behind schedule. Our engineering contractor had a fixed price contract and, when progress slipped, had failed to formulate the necessary recovery plan. I called in the managing director of the company and his senior management team.

I reinforced my team with people from my senior management to impress on them the seriousness of the situation: we had promised our customer we would finish by June.

We received assurances and something that was offered as a recovery plan. It was not a plan at all, just the original project schedule with the durations of all outstanding activities truncated to fit the time remaining; there was no detail of how this might become possible.

It was clear we could go faster but would not be able to complete on time. We had been keeping our business team informed and now urged them to inform the customer about the delay. They decided against this and Klaus was sent to assure the customer that we would be on time. This was a poor decision and not in keeping with our usual open and honest approach to business.

After repeated failures by the contractor to take action, I gave notice of termination of his contract; an action that would allow me to take over the work. However, I suspended this when he agreed to cooperate. I installed myself on site and insisted that the contractor appoint a member of his senior engineering management team to also be on site. What followed was an intensive campaign that cut the delay by half. The daily routine started with a morning meeting to look at the orders for the day and would always include me having to tell the contractor's senior manager that he was still not doing enough and was personally failing. When it became apparent that they were compromising on safety for speed and I had been unable to correct behaviour despite sustained efforts to get them to change, I had the contractor's start-up manager removed from the site and replaced. We got safety back under control and work continued at a good tempo.

When the customer realised that the required progress was not being made, a visit from a senior member of our team was demanded to explain. I became the lucky candidate and it was a very interesting experience.

A multi-wave dressing down had been organised in which one senior manager after another joined the meeting to inform me how unacceptable my behaviour had been and how my company's reputation could never recover. It was thorough and comprehensive. I was hung, drawn and quartered and the knowledge I was able to share with them about all the things being done to make fast, safe progress, did not divert them from their vitriol.

I was managing to take just a couple of hours off a week and I joined the Tees Rowing Club to preserve my sanity. I was able to borrow a single sculling boat and row up the Tees towards Yarm. Even in the summer the river looked cold. It was deep and peaty-brown, meandering laconically through fields and past woodlands. This provided a great tonic and very relaxing interlude a couple of times a week. Well, mostly relaxing. There was just the matter of passing the council estate at Thornaby where yobs with time on their hands enjoyed throwing rocks at a lone passing sculler, just to brighten their day. Either their aim was poor, or they weren't trying too hard to hit their target and I never took a direct hit. I felt uncomfortable about the yobs; not because I was their occasional target, but because it was sad to see the wasted potential (and perhaps to be reminded of my own council estate childhood).

I do not feel drawn towards the North East. Even on a July day when the sky is blue and the full warmth of the sun falls on your face, the breeze from the sea brings a chill that sends a shiver down your spine and reminds you how close you are – as the wind blows – to Siberia. Perhaps you have to be cold and aggressive to live here. Or is it the other way round?

We eventually got everyone going in the same direction and the plant was completed. The team had worked hard for long hours and, when we were in the commissioning phase, we worked around the clock.

The night after the day on which we had introduced feed gas, I was in the control room at 2am and I received a phone call from Matthew – a member of the commissioning team who would become the plant manager. He was calling in to check progress and to assess whether he could go home to bed. He had just left the hospital where his first child had been born. He just squeezed this extra mural activity between his commissioning responsibilities; such was the level of commitment of many people in our company.

When hydrogen was delivered to the customer, he began to warm to us. We had designed, built and commissioned the plant in 19½ months, which was world class performance, or better. I suppose the sales team had felt it appropriate, in order to secure the business, to be over optimistic about our ability to meet an impossibly short schedule. It did cause a lot of angst, but also brought out the best in the engineering team. This was not the only time I travelled home feeling I had been in a war.

I went back to my day job of leading the project management team and we were very active bidding and executing business. Engineers and support staff sat in open plan work areas and managers were allocated offices. I came to appreciate my office; it reduced distractions and allowed me to make the frequent – usually long – international phone calls that went with my job without disturbing others and it was useful for impromptu meetings with my staff. It also allowed me a space I could personalise with an ornament and a couple of pictures.

When we lived in Pennsylvania, I took a photograph of the children, then aged three and five. They were undressed in preparation for a bath and they wandered uninhibited into the lounge where I had just put a new film in my camera. The light was good and, as they stood with their backs to me with arms tenderly around each other, I took the picture.

I was using black and white film and it was one of those flukes when an amateur takes a professional looking picture – just the right amount of light and shadow. The innocence and affection – not always apparent between siblings – was captured. I framed the print and, all these years later when I was looking for a happy family picture for my office, selected this one. It hung there for a long time and I enjoyed the memories it carried when it occasionally caught my eye. Especially after a difficult telephone meeting, it would remind me of one of the important reasons for going to work.

One morning I had a visitor: the Director of Personnel. This was a man I knew quite well and we had enjoyed a good relationship. On this occasion he wore a serious expression and, in carefully measured phrases, explained that my picture was causing distress to a member of staff; not someone I worked with or even knew, but a woman from another part of the company who walked past my office on the way to her work place. It seemed she had been a victim of abuse as a child and the image that I had thought revealed only naïve beauty suggested something all together different to her. I was asked to remove it and I did, but with sadness. I was sad to lose my cherished image, uncomfortable that the adult world can have such a dark side and disappointed that an adult could not deal with her problem simply by not looking at something disagreeable to her.

We had paid off the mortgage by 2002 and were now comfortable financially, with salary growing and family costs decreasing. I no longer needed to work and considered early retirement. However, I was enjoying the work; I felt it was a privilege to have a position such as mine and I also felt I had a contribution to make.

There was a bit of shuffling of senior positions and I became the Regional Manager of the HyCO group, responsible for the engineering disciplines as well as the project management and proposal teams. We engineered and coordinated bids for new business and executed projects worth hundreds of millions of pounds. I was impressed that the company had given me this opportunity at an advanced stage of my career. This was a demonstration of commitment to the "Diversity Programme" that aimed to utilise the talents of all employees with no discrimination on grounds of gender, sexual persuasion, race or age. It was something of a reversal of a trend, especially in American companies, to favour younger managers who were perceived to have higher energy levels. A side effect was that business managers would sometimes particularly ask me to accompany them on visits to customers whom they thought might be more comfortable with a mature looking presence. "Take some grey hair," was the expression.

Our children had grown up and were busy with their own lives. Rowing had become a passion for me and I thought it a wonder that I, a man in my 50s, could compete at a high level in a strength and endurance sport. I was mostly racing men of my own age, but we were all very fit. My parents' generation would not have imagined this to be possible for them at the same age. They had not grown up with National Health orange juice and cod liver oil. Ours must be a golden age.

I never had to fight a war, working class children were nourished, an education was possible and there were some professions in which privilege was not necessary to get a job; a job in which one could reach one's potential. I had been able to earn enough money to bring up a family of four in comfort, to buy a house and have some savings. In fact, since we had modest tastes, Rosie and I had enough money to do anything we wanted to. Only time was a limitation.

I taught myself to scull. Single sculling is not easy; the boat is almost impossible to balance and, when you add the need to steer and apply maximum effort, it becomes a satisfying skill to acquire. I trained and raised my fitness to be equal or better than my competitors. When I participated in indoor rowing competitions, I would finish in the top three or four in Britain. In 2008 I failed to win by 0.3 seconds. On that occasion I had not been able to see the readout and did not realise how close I had been to winning. Had I worn my glasses I could, perhaps, have found another ounce of performance.

When I raced in the boat, I could beat average scullers, but I would sometimes find a competitor who was faster than I was. The difference was in the technique and, the more I learned about this, the more there was to it. To win at the better regattas needed power, skill and tactics. It is as important to think about not slowing the boat as much as trying. I took lessons from an ex-world champion, Allan Whitwell. I read books, I practised and I trained. I came to admire those who beat me and I got better until I was able to win the UK National Championship, Henley Veterans Regatta and other races in Britain, USA and Canada. Winning at the highest level required one further element: the management of pain. You can condition yourself to pain and you have to be prepared to live with substantial physical discomfort for most of the race.

Ultimately, you have to want to win more than your opposition does in order to manage the voices screaming at you to ease up. The top scullers were consistently able to win. I was never one of these, but occasionally on a good day when I managed to combine all the elements, I could beat them.

At one point I spent so much time in a single sculling boat – more time than I did walking – that the looking backwards seemed like the natural perspective; as in life, we can see where we have been and have an idea where we want to go, but we never have a clear view of the future.

I also competed in veterans' events in fours and eights. When I had rowed as a young man, the Ratzeburg Rudder Club had developed a successful technique using a long slide and they were prominent in international rowing. It was with satisfaction that I was in the Weybridge eight that overtook Ratzeburg in the Veteran's Head of the River Race. I liked to think that some members of the once dominant Ratzeburgers might have been in that boat.

A rowing, or rather sculling, experience that was particularly rewarding was the partnership I fell into with Derek Holmes, an amiable man, 12 years my senior. For those unfamiliar, a sculler has two oars, a rower one. At 6' 4" tall, Derek had the right physique. And he had the right attitude. We won many double scull events together, including the Boston Marathon. This is a race, held annually in September, over 31 miles from Boston to Lincoln along the drafty River Witham. We completed the course in just under four and a half hours after a solid paddle, interrupted only to carry the boat around Bardney Lock. We passed many younger crews, including men's eights, which are inherently much faster than a double.

215

It seemed that the tenacity of the older men outlasted the stamina of the younger ones. A race of this length is a memorable experience; it takes you through a number of stages of fatigue, each one more extreme than you could previously have imagined.

Finally, at the finish, we welcomed the help offered to lift the boat out of the water.

We both lay on the grass looking at the sky for around half an hour. It took this long for the body to remember that there are other positions possible than sitting in a racing boat, for the fluid and blood from hands where blisters had formed and been worn off to congeal, for blood to once again be sent to the brain instead of to essential rowing muscles and, finally, for the will to do anything to return. Then we had a cup of tea and went home; a very satisfying day out.

A little after this, Derek suggested we might row the Atlantic and this seemed like an adventure two ageing men might do while it was still possible. I gave it serious thought. I was busy at work, but supposed a sabbatical might have been negotiated. In the dark, early hours one morning, I awoke and thought about it. The voice in my head made comparisons: boat food – home cooking; seasick – land lubber; boat – bed; Derek – Rosie. I just didn't have what it would take.

In 2002 my rowing club had a good men's first eight of experienced rowers in their 20s and 30s. In February they were training for the Head of the River race from Mortlake to Putney and they needed a substitute for an outing. I sat in and they felt the boat had been better than with their regular four man. I stayed in the crew for the Head race and we finished in the first hundred. Not too bad. The Head has around 450 entries from top international crews as well as club crews. The last time I had done this race had been 33 years earlier when I had finished 86th.

The next phase of their season was to prepare for Henley Royal Regatta (HRR) and I was still in the crew. I was now in my late 50s and racing with the much younger men. We won enough regattas to make the cut and be selected for HRR. I was able to keep up with the training, but my body did protest and muscles would get scarred and knotted.

I discovered that a good sports masseur could fix that quite successfully. After a session of his treatment I was in my 20s again – for a while. We raced in the Thames Cup at HRR and were eliminated in the first round. Not a great result, although the nature of Henley seeding is such that we were paired with one of the top crews.

HRR is a wonderful study of privilege. It is organised by the Henley Stewards, which is a mysterious organisation. I hoped I would be invited to join, but an invitation never came and I had to apply. Sponsors were found and I wrote up my "contribution to rowing". I received a letter advising that, if I had raced at The Regatta, they would be pleased to accept £5 from me and put me on the waiting list. I could expect to wait about 7 years, they said. If I had not raced at The Regatta, they would accept a £50 deposit and I could expect to wait 15 years.

Membership of Stewards gives entry to the Stewards' Enclosure where you can rub shoulders with the great and the good, drink champagne and sleep in a deck chair at the water's edge. It is a good day out though and I love the eccentricity of it. There are bowler hatted marshalls to enforce the anachronistic rules and dress code. Gentlemen wear jackets and ties. Ladies wear dresses with hem lines below the knee (neck line can be as low as you like). We all strut around fully loaded with bonhomie and champers. Some watch the racing.

The Regatta runs like clockwork with every race starting on time. Every one of the marshalls, umpires, time keepers, launchmen and commentators knows their job. Those in good standing who have been able to execute their duties faultlessly in previous years may receive an invitation to officiate. A slip is likely to mean no invitation next year, but there would be no explanation, just a no letter on the mat.

It is a privilege to be in the inner sanctum of worthy individuals who are rewarded by the opportunity to do five days' unpaid work and the result is a perfectly organised and executed piece of history. This is the only case I can think of for privilege, which in all other situations is likely to fail to select the most able and is an impediment to social progress.

Rosie and I joined the National Trust. For my part this is not out of nostalgia for a richer time when people knew their place and the privileged were able to accumulate obscene wealth and exploit the majority, but to maintain the properties as memorials to the dark nature of those people in a, thankfully, past era – like the visitor centres at Auschwitz and Belsen. While we enjoy the riches of our heritage in Britain, we need to remember what can go wrong if we stop respecting each other. Rosie enjoys the gardens and restaurants where the food is always wholesome – much better than motorway services.

As a family we continued to be involved with the URC and I became an elder. I could never have imagined this as a possible path for me and, although I believe they are valuable and needed, I am still deeply suspicious of the mainstream religions. Like all human institutions – governments, companies, public services, trade unions – churches were established for honest reasons with good intentions, but their leaders forgot the reasons and started to serve only their own interests.

Charles Montesquieu, the inspiration of the Constitution of the United States of America, was thinking about this in the mid-eighteenth century and he declared, "In the realm of politics this is of the greatest consequence: constant experience shows us that every man invested with power is apt to abuse it and to carry his authority as far as it will go."

I think we have seen this in all religions, but my experience is only of Christianity in the Abrahamic line. In Judaism, clerics assumed a privileged position for themselves, closer to God than ordinary people. Then they told people that their race alone had been chosen by God; an attempt to create a monopoly in which the middlemen would further strengthen their role. This behaviour is not exclusive to Jewish clerics: it's a "middleman" thing.

It is not easy to find non-religious language to talk about this and religious language is a barrier to reaching people reluctant to consider the religious perspective. Let's just say a man came along who de-bunked the chosen race idea and explained that everyone could have the same access to God. A new church was founded on the ideas of this man, but a priestly cast again got their hands on it and we had threats, bullying, The Inquisition and selling of Indulgences. Later, we had protesters reminding us about the original message and they formed a new church – the Protestants. After a while this looked very much like the first group. Then people took back control and we had free churches in which the clerics are subordinated to the people – to the congregation. We have to watch the middlemen. Apart from the danger of corruption, they are inclined to resist change. Churches should lead or, at least keep up with social evolution. Ordinary people need to take responsibility and remind our clerics of the purpose of religion: to help our spiritual development and provide a moral compass that enables the building of a fair and secure society in which everyone has the opportunity to reach their potential.

We also have to watch ourselves. One of the corruptions religion is capable of is for a particular group to believe they have found the only true path. It is beyond our ability, at least with current knowledge, to know about matters of faith beyond doubt and we seem to make progress when are prepared to revise our knowledge as more is learned. Experience seems to show that when someone declares they alone are right, they have taken a wrong turn.

It has been a continuous struggle, but the Christian message of patience, respect and pluralism is so strong that it has survived and has provided the base for a society that has enabled its people to develop. Christianity has been the engine of development of our civilisation. Our liberal democracy is the natural product of this tradition.

Science has substantially replaced religion in explaining the universe, but it has also taught us how mysterious nature is. It is no longer necessary to think of God as supernatural but, like all of nature, just very difficult to understand. I don't think it has to be a choice between science and God. I choose science to help me understand physics and philosophy to help me understand people and God to put it all into a perspective from which I can begin to understand myself. Albert Einstein said, "Science without religion is lame; religion without science is blind." Newton saw order in the mechanics of the universe and took this as evidence of a creator. And he was not over impressed with his own achievements, saying, "I was like a boy playing on the beach and diverting myself now and then, finding a smoother pebble or a prettier shell than ordinary, whilst the great ocean of truth lay all undiscovered before me."

We could take a humanist, purely intellectual, view of life, but this may have a greater danger of pride and self delusion clouding our view and there are still mysteries too profound to be understood in just words and mathematics.

There is a spiritual dimension to life. I choose Christianity, but we need to look after it.

In my business life I continued the work I had been doing to grow the team and I recruited engineers for my department and others. Recruitment was difficult at this time with the engineering industry booming and there was strong competition for people at all levels.

I extended my horizons and recruited internationally and, by 2007 my group of forty people included ten nationalities, between them business fluent in sixteen languages. The atmosphere was fantastic in this melting pot of engineers who came from China and Ecuador and many places in between. The talent in that group was impressive and they worked hard, supporting each other to put together strong technical and commercial schemes as we bid and executed projects to build world class process plants.

I had learned that a manager's main responsibility is to create an environment in which all members of his team can be successful. This was the contribution I aspired to make.

I was travelling in support of new business and one of the countries I visited was Romania. I was initially shocked when I saw the poverty and decrepitness in that country. Everything was filthy and in disrepair. Feral dogs roamed the streets. When a member of our team was bitten and went to the hospital for treatment, he was stitched up and put on a course of anti-rabies drugs. He protested at first, having heard how unpleasant the side effects of the drugs can be. He was told simply, "Bring us the dog and we'll test that, otherwise you may die; rabies is not treatable once symptoms appear." We heard that a Japanese businessman had died earlier that year, from a dog attack in Bucharest.

I think the communist regime had invested well in education and I met competent engineers in Romania. That is, many had a good technical education, but they worked chaotically with no individual seemingly able to make decisions. Meetings were at a table 15 metres long around which sat dozens of engineers. Everything was referred up the line to the one man at the head of the table who decided everything.

The people I met in Romania were grey and languid with no enthusiasm or optimism. When I was able to speak privately to an individual he would tell me that nothing had changed since Ceausescu's downfall, which had been less than 20 years earlier and that the same people were still in charge; party members had simply become entrepreneurs and it would take a generation at least to see any movement.

My time in Romania was spent mostly in the industrial part of Constanta, a crumbling Black Sea resort, once favoured by Soviet party members and their families for summer holidays. I also had business in other cities, including Bucharest. One evening, at the end of a series of meetings over the previous few days, the members of the team from my company had dinner together. The native Romanian booked one of the few good restaurants in Bucharest for the six of us. We had representatives of the main functions of the business from operations, engineering and business management and, as we relaxed in anticipation of a pleasant meal, we noticed that we were all of different nationalities. I loved the diversity and the different viewpoints and expertise this brought. There were men from Romania, the Czech Republic, Germany, the USA, England (but from a Polish family and infused with that history and culture) and England (me).

We had all worked together from time to time and these people were good company. I remarked on this coming together of nationalities and we reflected on a Europe now closer to peace than at any time in the past. Then the German, in an unguarded, Freudian moment, looked at me and responded with, "When you started the war..."

I didn't have to say: "After you invaded Poland."

There was no need to articulate a reply. We six men seemed to share a stream of thought that contained sympathy for the victims of German aggression and for the German people who have to live with the crimes of their nation; recognition that none of us are much different and that criminals in our midst can mobilise if given the opportunity. We were all of generations sheltered from the full horror of war, but nevertheless touched by it, as we grew up in its aftermath, with people bearing its scars. We should be able to do better, much better. There was a pause while the concept was processed by this mini United Nations, then laughter that, again without words said, "We are happy we have all come to a better place in history and are optimistic that progress should continue." We drank a toast to Europe.

I took the Malaysia Airlines flight to Kuala Lumpur on the morning of 11 December 2008. Just after take-off from Heathrow, the plane banked north and east. This was just another flight, but it was long-haul and company travel policy allowed me the comfort of the business class cabin, so I sank into my seat to relax and slow down my metabolism and get some rest. I would check through my emails and urgent actions after breakfast. Looking out of the starboard window into the clear morning sky, I saw an enormous plume of black and grey smoke rolling and rising from somewhere in Hertfordshire.

My flight might have been routine, but what I was witnessing was not. It was very unusual, but viewed through the window it looked like a television report and not as tangibly real as an image of destruction on that scale should have been. It was probably obvious to anyone that this was a serious incident, but as an engineer experienced in the design and operation of process plant, I could see that this was a major event. I feared significant loss of life although this, surprisingly and thankfully, turned out not to be the reality.

I later learned that there had been an explosion at the Bunsfield oil storage depot. This led to criminal proceedings against five companies involved in the management and operation of the facility. There would be a thorough investigation and the efforts of people like me in the process industries would have another case study to learn from, bringing an opportunity to refocus our efforts on designing, building and operating such plant safely.

Safety is central to everything an engineer engaged in process plant design does and to the managers who guide the process. When something goes wrong, it is because we have failed and we study the investigation reports that are disseminated throughout the industry. The technical reasons are understood and revisions are made to the engineering standards that guide our work. The underlying cause of such failures is usually inadequate leadership; managers have failed to provide an environment in which adequately qualified and experienced engineers are able to do their jobs effectively. Ultimately, this flows from commercial pressure or indifferent executive leadership, but this is rare today and very different from the attitudes and practices that existed when I first entered a refinery in 1963. That said, there is still a lot of room for improvement and an ever present danger of complacency.

In the years I worked in engineering, there have been a few large scale disasters in the process and related industries: Flixborough in England (1974), Seveso in Italy (1976), Bopal in India (1984), Piper Alpha in the North Sea (1988), Texas City Refinery in the USA (2005), Bunsfield in England (2006) and Deepwater Horizon in the Gulf of Mexico (2011). The scale of the plants we build is always increasing with the obvious potential for greater consequences. The nuclear industry has a good record, but we have also seen the disasters of Three Mile Island in the USA (1979), Chernobyl in the Ukraine (1986) and Fukushima in Japan (2011).

This work can be done safely. It is the responsibility of engineers and managers, but also of those who drive the commercial frameworks of industry and those who consume. It is the responsibility of all of us to do ensure the work is done correctly.

Everyone wants the benefits of energy, fuels, gases, plastics and metals that are able to be produced at commercially acceptable costs. Indeed, society depends on these and the planet could not sustain its population of six billion and rising, without the contribution of engineers. All trades and professions are important in our interdependent modern society, but there is no profession more essential to society than engineering.

The group I managed was now responsible for a new hydrogen plant to be built near Kuala Lumpur to serve our business in Malaysia. We had a principle customer who would receive the gas by pipeline. He was in a hurry. I was travelling with the project manager, Adrian Bellaby, assigned to oversee the project and we would meet with the customer's General Manager, Medhani and his team.

A preparatory meeting in our offices had clarified what I had been concerned about: our business team had promised the customer he would have gas by the following December, but I had been over Bellaby's planning and I knew that this could not be achieved. It was also not what we had advised the business manager. However, she had judged that this was what the customer needed to hear in order to be persuaded to place the order with our company. This was not how we normally did business in Europe, but there was something of a frontier spirit in KL and her enthusiasm had affected her judgement.

Malaysia has three main ethnic groups: Malays, Chinese and Asians with the Malays accounting for just over 50%. Malays enjoy a number of privileges including reserved positions of state, land ownership rights and the ability to obtain certain business permits.

From my brief visit, it appeared that the work was done by the industrious Chinese and Asians while Malays occupied "management" positions.

Medhani was an intelligent, able and charismatic Asian who led his team of Chinese and Asians with authority; so much so, that they were all unable to tell him that his aspirations on schedule could not be achieved. We listened while Medhani's men, in turn, confirmed they would have their work done by the dates he demanded. Although I could see they had little more than optimism for believing this and we too could easily have told him what he wanted to hear – in the certainty that *we* would not be the cause of delay. I elected to be honest with him. This predictably caused an emotional reaction while he continued to play his game, but body language told me that he understood the reality. The relationship between us was good for the remaining phases of the project and we got the work done to his satisfaction.

After the meeting, Medhani entertained us to dinner, then the senior Chinese manager "allowed" us to take him on a tour of his favourite bars. This was a rich experience during which I learned that a favourite recreation for a Chinese Malaysian, or at least for this Chinese Malaysian, is to drink lots and lots of beer. Bellaby and I are both much bigger than most Chinese Malaysians and, as you might guess, may have more capacity to consume beer. However, these people clearly get a lot of practice. Quite a lot of my quota was used tactically, to "water" the indoor plants that decorated the bars and I was on duty after all - entertaining a customer. There seemed to be a different bar for each part of the evening. Around midnight we reached a bar full of Chinese men with a few girls.

We had now become familiar with the arrangement: about a dozen tables, each a metre in diameter on a high pillar so four or five people could stand, leaning on the table, while hostesses continually replenished the beer supply in large jugs, smiling and encouraging. By this time I was impressed by the capacity of these little men to keep drinking and none of them was showing any signs of weakening.

This was 17 December, or rather it had been 17 December when we started our binge. I was getting bored and started to think of home, wondering what Rosie would be doing. Absentmindedly, I glanced at my watch and mentioned to Bellaby that it was now my birthday. This turned out to be an error. Bellaby was a confident young man, capable of mischief. He appeared to excuse himself for a visit to the place where unwanted beer is discharged. On his way back to join us, he paused to chat to the bar owner who stood at the corner of the main bar keeping an eye on his staff, his girls and his customers to ensure that his operation ran smoothly and profitably.

"That's better," grunted Bellaby as he picked up his glass to start re-filling the space just made available.

I thought there was a slightly suspicious tightness to his smile. I put this down to bladder relief.

A few minutes later an attractive bar girl in a short skirt came up to me, poured me some more beer and smiled.

"You are tall. I like tall men."

Bar Owner interrupted the canned music and made an announcement over his sound system.

"We have a birthday. Have a happy birthday Mister – with compliments of Chin's Bar."

He was looking at me. Some of his customers were looking at me but, thankfully, most were concentrating on their beer.

The girl smiled and moved closer. As I said, I had been thinking of home a few minutes earlier. I'm not sure whether it was this, or just the realisation that it would be unwise to let Bellaby go back to the office with a tale of how he got his boss laid in KL. As politely as I could, I explained to the girl that I thought she was very attractive but I didn't want to be more friendly. She reported to Chin who looked across and nodded. Job done I thought, but it was only moments before a second girl joined our group.

"Hello, my name is Li. What's your name?"

I sent her back to Chin, asking her to thank him but say I didn't want a girl tonight. Receiving the news, Chin looked disappointed. He was clearly a man focused on customer satisfaction and he had made an announcement. That face-saving thing started to come into operation. He came over.

"Don't you like my girls? I have more."

I assured him, of course, that I did like his girls, but did not want one just now. He needed to be seen to complete the transaction and, after a little more negotiation, saved further difficulty by presenting me with a watch: Famous Grouse on the dial; made in Taiwan. I accepted with thanks.

The Chinese were still drinking. This was very impressive in a macho, bar sort of way and I wondered how this was possible. Then, restoring confidence in my ability to judge a person's beer capacity, I noticed a man at the table in the corner flop down; still standing, but apparently out cold, with face sideways on the table like a lump of dough. Then, hearteningly, another went down - and another. It seemed there was a genetic limit that they had all been determined to reach. They were now, at last, achieving their goal.

This was the signal we had been waiting for apparently and our "guests" signalled they were ready to go home. At this point we had two Chinese still with us: Medhani's man and a business associate we somehow picked up during the evening. The business associate said he could drop us at our hotel. This seemed a better option that Medhani's man who had passed out as he stepped into the outside air, before regaining consciousness and finding his car.

During the few days we had spent in Malaysia, people had frequently been at pains to point out to us all the British features they had retained in their country: driving on the left, the electrical sockets, the legal system and Scotch Whisky. We had now come to understand that they could also emulate British drink driving standards of the sixties – Malaysia became independent in 1957 and, perhaps, had not copied legislation after that date.

Business Associate drove with wheels straddling the white line, explaining that he could not otherwise follow the road. It seemed sensible. It seemed sensible at the time. Reflecting on it in the morning it seemed less sensible, although this little bit of recklessness echoing pre-nanny state days felt just a little bit liberating.

When I got home Rosie agreed the watch had been a good choice.

Chapter 20

Time to Go

I am sure I made a good contribution to the business, to our engineering standards, to the recruitment and development of staff and to our relationships with the organisations we worked with in partnership. I was able to influence our global engineering organisation to some extent, but I was also feeling increasingly out of step with the direction of the company. I honestly believe I was always loyal to my bosses and to the company, but sometimes my questioning of decisions and plans from the top seemed to be interpreted as opposition. I eventually decided, at the end of 2007, that the time had come to retire. I gave notice of my intention and worked a year's notice to ensure a smooth transition.

When I decided to retire, I had been concerned that the time was not good for the company. We were busy and needed all the resources possible. By the time I actually left, however, the situation had dramatically reversed and, within another half year, colleagues were being forced into early retirement or redundancy.

The world's financial system had collapsed and I think we could see that the government, now led by Gordon Brown, had not been as prudent as my mum would have been. There was nothing in the store cupboard. Spending had increased on social programmes and, although advances were being made, there was waste. Keynesian economics had worked for post-war governments, but clearly there had to be a limit to debt. It was not surprising that the political pendulum should swing again.

Although Gordon Brown shared responsibility for running up the national debt to levels that could only be manageable if economic prosperity could be guaranteed, we should be grateful to him for his competent corrective action after the melt down of the banking system, which was a global event. It is one of the cruelties of politics that he is remembered as the prime minister at the time of the crisis and not for his leadership, which followed by the world's governments, limited the extent of the catastrophe.

We need government and opposition and it is healthy that this changes from time to time, but I think many of our politicians on both sides of the political divide know that we need a fundamental change, perhaps a realignment of political parties, but how to achieve this evades them. It seems obvious that many of the Conservative values that worked in an age before democracy are no longer appropriate, although we may be able to preserve some valuable elements such as self-reliance and appropriate reward for innovation. We do need to eliminate privilege, which allows unfair advantage for some families, individuals and professions.

At the heart of Conservative philosophy is the confidence that an intelligent, responsible and capable elite will act as stewards of the standards and wealth of the nation. The belligerent and unsympathetic response to the 1984 miners' strike and repeated attacks on education, health and other public services have revealed the lie to this. Also, it just doesn't seem democratic to allow an elite minority to accumulate obscene amounts of wealth and enjoy the influence that goes with this. It's not going to be acceptable to the majority and crime and social unrest are bound to follow.

The practical weakness of an elitist politic is its failure to engage the majority of our people. It may have worked when Britain controlled a large part of the globe and undemocratic, elitist government was possible, but it is not very good when we have to compete on equal terms with independent emerging economies. We now need to educate, empower and engage all our people. We need to move on.

It should be within our capability to do much better and there are plenty of case studies that we can draw on, some partially successful, some mostly unsuccessful, but the data is there to be used. The first step should surely be to agree values that embrace a common view of the society we aspire to. There is probably enough experience from the political systems that have been tried to be able to design one that would serve the needs of a liberal, democratic and dynamic society in the next period of our social evolution. It probably cannot be achieved in one nation alone, but will need a consensus across nations and will therefore be slow. I am optimistic enough to believe that this is what is actually happening as society evolves.

The American Declaration of Independence gives us some of the basic principles: "We hold these truths to be self-evident, that all men are created equal, that they are endowed by their Creator with certain unalienable Rights, which among these are Life, Liberty and the pursuit of Happiness. To secure these rights, Governments are instituted among Men, deriving their just powers from the consent of the governed." Further, the basis of the US system of government with its checks and balances looks like a good place to start and should not be rejected just because it was inspired by a Frenchmen – Charles Montesquieu – who, in 1748, argued that the best way to secure liberty and prevent a government from becoming corrupted was to divide the powers of government among different groups of officials who would check each other.

We can also learn from the mistakes of the USA. Its constitution has some good elements and is subject to revision as the times demand, but has been followed only selectively and has led to the most unequal society on the planet. The treatment of native people and black slaves, the only use of nuclear weapons against civilians and the profligate pollution of the planet must rank among the worst abuses in human history.

In the Russian experiment with communism, we have seen the dangers of absolute, centralised power in a godless society. The varieties of human nature could not be accommodated and dissention had to be eliminated. Innovation was stifled, people were disengaged and the system eventually imploded.

The other great lesson of the 20th century was Nazi Germany, which showed what a master race could be capable of.

So, we'll need agreed values and a constitution. The things we need to agree on are whether we need to avoid privilege, encourage self reliance and avoid a benefit culture; whether we want equal opportunity and access to education with opportunity for intellectual and spiritual development; whether we want to value all work, including labour and whether to reward innovation and service. Also whether we think we need to respect each other at work and at home and support the vulnerable. We will have to address the question of how to provide an appropriate level of medical care. We will probably agree on the desirability of security from internal and foreign threats.

When the values are agreed, it should be straightforward to write a constitution. Politicians can offer their policies and taxes can be designed to encourage behaviour that supports the values and avoids the unwanted side effect of reducing the incentive to work. The constitution will have to be adjusted as we measure our progress.

Chapter 21

The Beginning

Mum had been suffering from osteoporosis and in April, a few months after I retired, a couple of vertebrae collapsed and rendered her almost immobile in great pain. Up to that point I had been impressed by the ability of the National Health Service to provide what I had observed to be such comprehensive treatment to so many people. However, I suppose, the sheer weight of numbers of old people who have outlived their bodies can eventually overwhelm it.

Mum was taken by ambulance to Southampton General Hospital. Her GP had declined to attend her when friends called to report her condition. I joined her in the hospital where we waited for a day to receive a cursory examination and, when she managed with the help of a Zimmer frame and with tears of pain streaming down her face, to walk to the toilet, she was declared fit to go home alone. It needed all my intellect and business experience to stumble to an understanding of how the care system is supposed to work. I had no hesitation about paying for help, but it was bureaucracy that was the barrier and not money. I brought her home to live with Rosie and me so we could ensure she received whatever help was able to be procured. I was grateful for the care we were able to get from my GP, Dr. Arnold (perhaps we have less geriatrics in my area, or perhaps we were just lucky to have an exceptional GP).

I paid for a scan and arranged a consultation with a spinal specialist. We saw him at 4 pm on a Friday afternoon. He was an enigmatic character. He examined Mum and consulted the scan and x-ray results.

"You're my worst nightmare on a Friday afternoon," he said, "I don't know where to begin."

After what appeared to be careful thought, he advised, taking care to inform us that he did not see a good outlook, that we should see a colleague of his who might be able to construct scaffolding around the broken vertebrae. His colleague was in Southampton General where they have better facilities than we have in Surrey, apparently! Mum seemed quite cheered by her consultation.

"He was very direct. I can do business with a man like that," she said dryly.

We took her home and continued with Dr. Arnold's supervision to adjust the drugs, attempting to manage the pain. After about six weeks the pain did, in fact, decrease to a level that allowed Mum to clear her head and she became quite cheerful. We felt we were getting somewhere and with a chance of some improvement. Mum went to bed on 17 August saying her leg was uncomfortable in a new way. The next morning I slept unusually late. Rosie had got up and, realising Mum had been in the bathroom for some time, became concerned. Mum had lain down on the floor and died from what the post mortem revealed was a pulmonary embolism – a blood clot.

Despite the circumstances, we had had a rewarding time together in the summer of 2009. Mum and I got to know each other – to know each other as adults. It felt different from our relationship over the years that consisted of day visits and short stays. She was able to see the people Rosie and I had become in a modern globe-trotting world, quite distant from Mum's world in The Forest. We were able to listen to her stories with time to understand and appreciate what sort of people my parents had been. All our children and grandchildren visited several times and there was the giving and receiving love.

After my war, on my birthday – these were coming fast now – a year after retiring, I was reading the book my daughter Katie gave me as a present: *The Last Veteran – Harry Patch and the Legacy of War*. Reading about the memories of WW1 survivors, of how they felt at the armistice; wearied and relieved. I felt I had experienced my own war: years of relentless pressure in an all-absorbing battle to survive and (sometimes win) in the corporate battlefield. I had seen comrades give their all. Mine was not a fighting war, but it was a long campaign in which energy, courage, resourcefulness and support of wonderful people were necessary and a successful outcome had not always been the predictable conclusion.

One success was our family. We had brought up four children who had matured into decent adults. Decent adults who respect and support each other and we are all good friends: Rosie, Finbarr, Kiera, Katie, Edward and me. It was a long road that we navigated with tools we inherited – some remembered from the examples of our parents and some baked into our intuition – and with things we had learned from good people along the way.

Words are the tools I use to think with. Sometimes I can find words to give an impression of what is important to me and how I feel about the world. I feel the words I have collected and organised in these pages may tell others who I am. They also express how I feel about my wife and how we fit together.

When I try to write about the children, I am unable to find suitable words and this may be because they have been so many different people – each of them – from snivelling infant and happy baby, enthusiastic child and surly youth to inconsistent student and complex young adult. I have wanted them to be like me, but more conscientious, more considerate and with greater success.

They should have earned doctorates at the best universities before becoming surgeons, prime ministers and scientists – as well as being athletes taking Olympic honours along the way. I hoped for them to find partners like my partner.

I think I have learned that parenting is just like engineering management: the main responsibility is to create an environment in which the people (in this case the children) can reach their potential.

I realise now that they are all wonderful new people made from our soup, nourished by the love Rosie and I have given them, influenced by the time and places we put them in – and damaged by the errors we have made. They are the family I would have ordered – if that was the way children were procured. I love them more for being themselves and for being more than I could have imagined. They will have to tell their own stories in their own words.

Now we have time to reflect and to be together, Rosie and I are beginning to understand each other and ourselves. There are no regrets; there is no desire to be young again. It's been a journey and we have arrived – or are nearing our destination. Like a rowing competition. We needed to do all that training and endure the pain of the big race to be able to earn that feeling: we would not be at that point with the satisfaction of having achieved something if we had not made the effort.

Rosie and I have made the effort. At first in retirement, like my dad, I felt guilt that I was receiving income without working. I have come to see it more as the satisfying part when the race is done.

Of course, there is always another race.

I could not have anticipated what being retired would be like until I began to experience it. Perhaps I had an idea it would be a life of unlimited time in which to choose what I would do, a pleasurable absence of commands from others, only some of which were in step with my own ideas; perhaps a sad missing of valued colleagues and interesting engineering and business stimulation. Except for the "unlimited time", it is all of these, but something I hardly expected was the gift to see and experience my wife anew.

Not just a mate, mother of my children, warmer of my bed, keeper of my house, friend to walk with, talk with, but now much more; the bride of my youth returned to me, soul mate, fellow traveller in space and time and sharer of dreams. More than 40 years of shared toils, joys, disappointments and successes have kept us too busy to savour life, to dwell in our love, even to really know each other, but these shared tests have laid a road with a base so solid and a finish so smooth that, when I look at it now and start to feel its quality, I see we are ready for a cruise to the stars and beyond. Our journey is just beginning.

Since our species first gained self-awareness that gave us an antenna able to receive information from the entire universe and perceive its beauty, wonder and opportunity, we have been sustained by it. We have also been able to contribute to its intricate tapestry.

When we think or when we act we add something, good or bad, to the fabric of existence and when we feel optimistic and right with the world, we are drawing on the good stuff put there by all the people in all the generations since the very beginning. I am blessed with a soul mate of sweet nature and, perhaps, more tuned than many to this. It warms me and makes me better, stronger, richer. It even feels that I have become more able to add some threads.

Whatever happens to Rosie or to me, our love will always be in the fabric and cannot be lost; it will always be there for our children to draw on, or for anyone to feel if they wish. It is not ours alone but belongs to the tapestry.

240

Lightning Source UK Ltd.
Milton Keynes UK
UKOW051423080512

192159UK00004B/28/P